THE DEVELOPMENT OF MIRROR SELF-RECOGNITION IN DIFFERENT SOCIOCULTURAL CONTEXTS

Joscha Kärtner, Heidi Keller, Nandita Chaudhary, and Relindis D. Yovsi

W. Andrew Collins
Series Editor

MONOGRAPHS OF THE SOCIETY FOR RESEARCH IN CHILD DEVELOPMENT

Serial No. 305, Vol. 77, No. 4, 2012

 Boston, Massachusetts   Oxford, United Kingdom

EDITOR
W. ANDREW COLLINS
University of Minnesota

MANAGING EDITOR
ADAM MARTIN
Society for Research in Child Development

EDITORIAL ASSISTANT
LAURA KOZMINSKI
Society for Research in Child Development

Board of Advisory Editors

Brian K. Barber
University of Tennessee

Michael P. Maratsos
University of Minnesota

Glenn I. Roisman
University of Illinois

Kathleen Thomas
University of Minnesota

Manfred Van Dulmen
Kent State University

Thomas Weisner
University of California, Los Angeles

Philip David Zelazo
University of Toronto

EDITORIAL CONSULTANTS

Emma K. Adam
Northwestern University

Mark Appelbaum
University of California, San Diego

Richard Aslin
University of Rochester

Marian Bakermans-Kranenburg
Leiden University

John Bates
Indiana University

Nazli Baydar
Koc University

Theodore Beauchaine
University of Washington

Susan Branje
Utrecht University

Celia Brownell
University of Pittsburgh

Melissa M. Burch
Hampshire College

Susan Campbell
University of Pittsburgh

Stephanie Carlson
University of Minnesota

Jane Childers
Trinity University

Gregory Cook
University of Wisconsin-Whitewater

Joan Cook
University of Wisconsin-Whitewater

Susan Crockenberg
University of Vermont

Pamela Davis-Kean
University of Michigan

Jacquelynne Eccles
University of Michigan

James Elicker
Purdue University

Michelle M. Englund
University of Minnesota

Kurt Fischer
Harvard University

Doran French
Illinois Wesleyan University

Sarah Friedman
CNA Corporation

Douglas Frye
University of Pennsylvania

Andrew Fuligni
University of California, Los Angeles

Susan Graham
University of Calgary

Elena Grigorenko
Yale University

Megan Gunnar
University of Minnesota

Paul Harris
Harvard University

Susan Hespos
Vanderbilt University

Aletha Huston
University of Texas, Austin

Lene Jensen
Clark University

Ariel Kalil
University of Chicago

Melissa Koenig
University of Minnesota

Brett Laursen
Florida Atlantic University

Eva Lefkowitz
Pennsylvania State University

Katherine Magnuson
University of Wisconsin, Madison

Ann Masten
University of Minnesota

Kevin Miller
University of Michigan

Ginger Moore
Pennsylvania State University

David Moshman
University of Nebraska

Darcia Narvaez
University of Notre Dame

Katherine Nelson
City University of New York

Lisa Oakes
University of California, Davis

Thomas O'Connor
University of Rochester

Yukari Okamoto
University of California, Santa Barbara

Robert Pianta
University of Virginia

Mark Roosa
Arizona State University

Karl Rosengren
University of Illinois, Urbana-Champaign

Judith G. Smetana
University of Rochester

Kathy Stansbury
Morehouse College

Steve Thoma
University of Alabama

Michael Tomasello
Max Planck Institute

Deborah Vandell
University of California, Irvine

Richard Weinberg
University of Minnesota

Hirokazu Yoshikawa
New York University

Qing Zhou
Arizona State University

THE DEVELOPMENT OF MIRROR SELF-RECOGNITION IN DIFFERENT SOCIOCULTURAL CONTEXTS

CONTENTS

ABSTRACT	vii
INTRODUCTION	1
METHOD	24
RESULTS	37
DISCUSSION	66
REFERENCES	81
ACKNOWLEDGMENTS	87
CONTRIBUTORS	88
STATEMENT OF EDITORIAL POLICY	89
SUBJECT INDEX	91
AUTHOR INDEX	98

ABSTRACT

The overarching goal of the present study was to trace the development of mirror self-recognition (MSR), as an index of toddlers' sense of themselves and others as autonomous intentional agents, in different sociocultural environments. A total of 276 toddlers participated in the present study. Toddlers were either 16, 17, 18, 19, 20, or 21 months old at their first assessment and completed weekly MSR assessments over a period of 6 weeks ($N = 1,577$). The toddlers and their families were from one of four sociocultural contexts: A prototypical autonomous sociocultural context (urban German middle-class families, $n = 82$), two prototypical relational sociocultural contexts (rural Indian and rural Nso families living in subsistence-based ecologies, $n = 54$ and $n = 80$, respectively), or an autonomous-relational sociocultural context (urban Indian middle-class families, $n = 60$). In line with previous research, we hypothesized that the onset of MSR would be earlier in sociocultural contexts in which mothers value and support their toddlers' development of autonomy. In addition, we considered three factors that covary with culture and that might compromise the cross-cultural validity of MSR as a behavioral measure of toddlers' sense of themselves as independent agents: familiarity with mirrors, culture-specific norms of expressive behavior, and motivation for tactile exploration. Finally, we analyzed toddlers' reactions to their specular image (e.g., pointing, playmate, and experimenting behavior) across time and culture as well as their relation to MSR. The results indicate that MSR increased with age in all sociocultural contexts. In line with our hypotheses, MSR rates were higher in the autonomy-supporting cultural context (urban German, urban Indian) than they were in the relational cultural contexts (rural Indian, rural Nso). The sociocultural differences in MSR could not, however, be explained by differences in mirror familiarity or culture-specific norms of expressive behavior. The cross-cultural validity of MSR as an index of toddlers' sense of themselves as independent agents is further supported by positive associations between MSR and pronoun use in all sociocultural contexts. Cross-cultural variation in MSR could best be explained by caretakers' emphasis on autonomous socialization goals, followed by toddlers' motivation for tactile exploration. These findings enhance our current understanding of development in more general terms by adding one more puzzle piece to the emerging picture of culture-specific developmental pathways. In order to understand developmental processes, one must take into account caretakers' cultural models and exercise caution when generalizing beyond the specific sociocultural context at hand.

INTRODUCTION

There are fundamental developmental achievements in the sociocognitive and socioemotional domains that take place during the second year of life. At about 18 months of age, toddlers start to differentiate between their own and others' psychological states and gain some understanding of the subjective nature of individuals' preferences (Repacholi & Gopnik, 1997) and interests (Tomasello & Haberl, 2003). At this age, toddlers also begin to anticipate and act on the emotions of others (Bischof-Köhler, 1991; Johnson, 1982; Zahn-Waxler, Radke-Yarrow, Wagner, & Chapman, 1992) and show the first signs of embarrassment and pride (Kagan, 1981; Lewis, Sullivan, Stanger, & Weiss, 1989). Most researchers argue that it is the development of the self and self-other differentiation that makes each of these developmental advances possible. As soon as toddlers have an awareness of themselves as autonomous agents who have subjective states (i.e., separate and independent beings), they infer that other people also have their own, separate lives by observing their behavior (e.g., facial expressions and object-directed behavior).

Researchers have traditionally measured the emergence of self-awareness and self-other differentiation using mirror self-recognition (MSR), a task that was first described by Gallup (1970) and Amsterdam (1972). In developmental psychology, the standard procedure for assessing MSR involves surreptitiously marking an individual's face in a way that the mark cannot be seen in the individual's peripheral vision. Individuals are subsequently shown a mirror and their behavior toward the mirror is observed. In most studies, mark-directed behavior is defined as the central criterion for passing the MSR task; toddlers must touch the mark on their face (or touch/ retrieve a sticker attached to their hair or legs) in order to pass the test. The rigidity of behavioral criteria and tolerance vary across studies, however (see also Bard, Todd, Bernier, Love, & Leavens, 2006). Specifically, there are differences in the definition of mark-directed behavior (e.g., whether toddlers had to touch the mark exactly, touch the vicinity of the mark, or simply touch their face with an extended index finger), whether or not toddlers had to look at their specular image while showing mark-directed behavior, and whether or not toddlers qualified as self-recognizers when they said their name, indicated verbally that something was different about their marked face, stared at the marked face, or showed self-referential pointing gestures (for an overview see Table 1).

THE MEANING OF MSR

Over the last 40 years, different meanings have been attributed to MSR. On the one hand, there are parsimonious interpretations that define MSR as nothing more than the matching of visual and kinesthetic information (e.g., Mitchell, 1993). On the other hand, some researchers interpret successful MSR as an indicator of the capacity to introspect and reflect on one's own mental states and, consequently, to understand the mental states of others as well (e.g., Gallup, 1983, 1998). Both of these positions are, however, hard to defend given the amount of disconfirming empirical evidence that has accumulated over the last three decades.

In fact, most of the recent research on MSR supports the intermediary position that MSR is an indicator of an early self-concept that implies some kind of representation of the self. Some authors have suggested that MSR is an indication of toddlers' understanding that the image in the mirror is a representation of their physical features (Nielsen, Suddendorf, & Slaughter, 2006; Povinelli & Cant, 1995). For example, Nielsen et al. (2006) reported that toddlers aged 18 and 24 months touched a sticker at equivalent rates regardless of whether the sticker was placed on their leg or on their face. If, however, the appearance of the toddlers' legs had been changed before marking by surreptitiously slipping the child into a novel pair of pants fixed to a highchair, most toddlers failed the leg-recognition task. Toddlers who were given a direct 30-s exposure to the modified appearance of their legs before the sticker was applied touched the stickers on their legs and faces at equivalent rates. Thus, self-recognizers seem to be able to form and update a representation of their whole body. A recent study by Moore, Mealiea, Garon, and Povinelli (2007) corroborated this finding; their results indicate that there is a correlation between MSR and body self-awareness that is independent of age. In their study, Moore at al. found that toddlers were more likely to step off a mat that was attached to the back of a child's shopping cart when they were asked to push the cart forward. In this way, the authors argued that self-recognizers were more likely to realize that their body formed an obstacle for reaching a goal.

Whereas some researchers are careful not to let their interpretations of MSR go beyond representations of the physical features of the self, others favor interpretations of MSR that indicate awareness of psychological states (e.g., emotions, volitions, desires). For these researchers, successful performance on MSR tasks is evidence that toddlers have a representation of the self and others not only as physical beings but as autonomous agents who have

TABLE 1

EMPIRICAL FINDINGS CONCERNING MSR: STUDY CHARACTERISTICS AND SELF-RECOGNITION RATES AS A FUNCTION OF AGE (MONTHS)

Reference	Sociocultural Context and Age	Criteria for MSR	Percentage of Self-Recognizers in Each Age-Group			
			12–14	15–17	18–20	21–24
Cross-sectional Studies						
Amsterdam (1972)	White; 2/3 middle-class, 1/3 lower class 18–20 months 21–24 months	Touch dot, say name, point to self			42	63
Schneider-Rosen & Cicchetti (1984)	White lower-class (50% maltreated) 18.2–20.7 months	Touch nose while looking at reflection			41	
Priel & de Schonen (1986)	Urban middle-class and Bedouin nomadic 13–19 months 20–26 months	Manipulate mark		15–20		80–85
Schneider-Rosen & Cicchetti (1991)	1/3 lower-class; 1/3 middle-class; 1/3 maltreated	Touch nose while looking at reflection, say name			32	73
Asendorpf & Baudonnière (1993)	White middle-class 18.6–19.6 months	Attempt to touch mark, including corresponding part on left side of face			52	
Asendorpf et al. (1996)	White middle-class 18.2–18.9 months	Attempt to touch mark, including corresponding part on left side of face			45	
Lewis & Ramsay (1997)	European-American middle-class 17.4–20.7 months	Touch nose, say name			62	

TABLE 1
CONTINUED

Reference	Sociocultural Context and Age	Criteria for MSR	Percentage of Self-Recognizers in Each Age-Group			
			12–14	15–17	18–20	21–24
Harel et al. (2002)	White middle-class 20 months	Touch nose, say name			~65	
Courage et al. (2004)	White middle-class 15–23 months	Touch nose while viewing mirror image		40	73	90
Nielsen et al. (2006)[1]	White middle-class 17.5–19.1 months 22.3–25.5 months	Touch or reach within 2 cm of the sticker			42	87
Herold & Akhtar (2008)	80% white, college graduates 17.6–20.6 months	Touch nose while looking at reflection			60	
Longitudinal Studies						
Lewis & Brooks-Gunn (1979): Expt 1	Euro-American (upper) middle-class 9.2, 12.3, 15.3, 18.3, 21.2, 24.1 months	Touch nose, verbal reference to change	0	19	25	69–80
Lewis & Brooks-Gunn (1979): Expt 2	Euro-American (upper) middle-class 14.5–18.1 months 20.7 – 24.4 months	Touch nose, verbal reference to change		33		67
Lewis et al. (1985)	Middle- to upper middle-class 18[c], 24[c] months	Mark-directed behavior			46	70

TABLE 1
CONTINUED

Reference	Sociocultural Context and Age	Criteria for MSR	Percentage of Self-Recognizers in Each Age-Group			
			12-14	15-17	18-20	21-24
Nielsen et al. (2003)	Not specified	Touch mark while looking at reflection (max = 2 cm off mark)	~5	~30	64	~85-92
Nielsen & Dissanayake (2004)	12[a], 15[a], 18[a], 21[a], 24[a] months White middle-class Biweekly from 15 to 23 months					
Courage et al. (2004)	White middle-class	Touch nose, verbal reference to change		30	75	100
Lewis & Ramsay (2004)	White middle-class 15[b], 18[b], 21[b], 24[b] months	Touch nose		11	47	82-100

Note. [1]Percentages are mean scores of study 1-3 without "no exposure" condition; [a]1-month range; [b]±2 weeks; [c]±1 month.

subjective feelings and experiences. With regard to self-awareness, there is empirical evidence that MSR correlates with self-conscious emotions such as embarrassment (Lewis et al., 1989; see also Amsterdam, 1972) and pronoun use (Courage, Edison, & Howe, 2004; LeVine, 1983; Lewis & Ramsay, 2004). According to the co-emergence hypothesis, other-awareness (the understanding that other people are also autonomous agents with their own psychological states) emerges simultaneously with self-awareness (e.g., de Waal, 2008a, 2008b). The emergence of other-awareness is implicit in the correlation between MSR and embarrassment described above: Being embarrassed at the sight of one's specular image implies not only self-awareness but also other-awareness in the sense that toddlers understand how they themselves appear to others (Barresi & Moore, 1996; Rochat & Zahavi, 2011). Further support for the co-emergence hypothesis comes from studies showing that MSR correlates with synchronous imitation (Asendorpf & Baudonnière, 1993; Asendorpf, Warkentin, & Baudonnière, 1996) and other types of social imitation (Hart & Fegley, 1994). MSR has also been shown to correlate with empathically motivated prosocial behavior (Bischof-Köhler, 1989, 1994; Kärtner, Keller, & Chaudhary, 2010; Zahn-Waxler et al., 1992), level-1 perspective taking, and learning novel actions from third-party interaction (Herold & Akhtar, 2008). Importantly, these correlations are independent of age (with the exception of Lewis et al., 1989) and have medium to large effect sizes (rs range between .21 and .68). In this way, MSR and other indicators of self- and other-awareness do not correlate simply because they are both age-dependent but because there is a conceptual relation between the mechanisms underlying their developmental emergence.

After integrating all of the findings on different developmental advances that occur around the middle of the second year, Perner (1991) proposed that there is a domain-general change in representational capacity, that is, secondary representation (see also Suddendorf & Whiten, 2001). According to this theory, children can construct multiple secondary representations of the future, past, or hypothetical events that make all the aforementioned developmental advances possible (e.g., self-awareness, imitation, empathic concern). For example, body self-awareness requires a secondary representation of one's own body and its spatiotemporal relation to the environment.

Building on the concept of secondary representation, Barresi and Moore (1996) proposed an intentional schema that allows infants from the age of 18 months to integrate first-person information (i.e., subjective awareness of directed activity) and third-person information (i.e., observed movements, object-directed behavior, facial expressions). The result is a representation that links an agent to an object through an intentional relation. As a consequence, secondary representations allow toddlers to infer the third-person information of their own subjective awareness and the first-person information from others' observed behavior. For example, being embarrassed requires a representation of one's own outer appearance and how it appears to others, and feeling empathy requires a secondary representation of the internal state of the person in need. According to Moore (2007), the development of imagination and self-other distinction allows children to understand themselves and others as separate beings; children develop an awareness of their independence and conceive of themselves and others as autonomous, intentional agents. There are a number of studies that have shown that MSR develops at a similar age as many other developmental attainments that are associated with secondary representations. For example, in two studies with age-homogenous samples, MSR was correlated with pretend play (Lewis & Ramsay, 2004; Nielsen & Dissanayake, 2004). Furthermore, toddlers begin to understand the subjectivity of preferences and interests at around the same age, in the middle of the second year (Repacholi & Gopnik, 1997; Tomasello & Haberl, 2003).

In contrast to the secondary representation hypotheses, Mitchell's (1993) visual-kinesthetic matching account excludes any idea of secondary representation in favor of an association between two primary representations—visual (specular image) and kinesthetic information—that enables MSR. This theory may suffice as an explanation of MSR, but only if one examines the development of MSR in isolation. As soon as one takes into account any of the aforementioned correlations between MSR and other manifestations of self- and other-awareness, visual-kinesthetic matching seems too narrow an explanation for MSR.

At the same time, it is important to note that it is unlikely that toddlers' emerging awareness of their own and others' psychological states leads to an immediate, full-blown capacity of these toddlers to contemplate their own and others' mental or psychological states as Gallup (1983, 1998) suggested. Today, there is ample evidence that this kind of metarepresentation only develops at the age of 3 or 4 years (Perner, 1991). We propose that, based on secondary representation, toddlers' subjective experience of inner states changes during their second year; from then on, toddlers differentiate between self and others' psychological states and perceive their inner states as their own, subjective experience that is located within, or bound to, their own bodies.

WHAT IS THE SECONDARY REPRESENTATION IN MSR?

Researchers have offered a variety of explanations for the secondary representation that is involved in MSR. Baudonnière et al. (2003) suggested, similar to Perner (1991) and others, that toddlers must associate their specular image (primary representation) and a (secondary) representation of their own face or body that they cannot see directly in order to succeed at self-recognition (Asendorpf & Baudonnière, 1993; Asendorpf et al., 1996; Harel, Eshel, Ganor, & Scher, 2002; Nielsen et al., 2006). Bischof-Köhler (1989), in contrast, argues that it is the association between the specular image (primary representation) and kinesthetic self-awareness (secondary representation) that predicts successful MSR performance (see also Barth, Povinelli, & Cant's [2004] notion of SELF). Both of these approaches identify an important aspect of MSR: There needs to be a comparison between one's specular image and a secondary representation of one's own physical appearance in order to notice any difference in appearance (e.g., a novel mark). Furthermore, there has to be an association between the specular image and kinesthetic self-awareness that enables the individual to locate and touch the spot. There are caveats to each of these approaches, however; Baudonnière et al. (2003) and Perner (1991) do not take into account how the toddlers know where to touch themselves and Bischof-Köhler (1989) and Barth et al. (2004) do not take into account how the toddlers know that there is something different when looking at their specular image. In our opinion, MSR necessitates the association of all three representations: The perceived specular image (primary representation) has to be integrated with the (secondary) representation of the toddlers' physical appearance and the toddlers' kinesthetic self-awareness (secondary representation).

Taken together, there is good empirical evidence that MSR is an appropriate indicator of toddlers' capacity to build specific types of secondary representations (see also Baudonnière et al., 2003) that enable them to conceive of themselves and others as autonomous agents with subjective internal states. In addition, unlike other potential indicators of self- and other-awareness (e.g., self-conscious emotions, pronoun use, synchronous imitation), MSR correlates with most of the other potential indicators of self-other awareness. It is for these reasons that, in the present study, we decided to use MSR as the central empirical measure in order to examine more closely the emergence of an early sense of self and others.

ONTOGENETIC DEVELOPMENT OF MSR

It has now been well established that MSR develops between 15 and 24 months of age (for an overview see Table 1). Specifically, recognition rates are below 35% for toddlers younger than 18 months of age but between the ages of 18 and 20 months, recognition rates increase to 40–65%. By the time toddlers are 21 to 24 months old, recognition rates reach 60–95%. With regard to gender differences, boys and girls show similar MSR rates in all studies listed in Table 1 except two studies that found that MSR rates were significantly higher for girls than they were for boys (Asendorpf & Baudonnière, 1993; Herold & Akhtar, 2008).

As shown in Table 1, the age of emergence (AOE) of MSR (as measured by the mean age of first-time recognizers) reported in some longitudinal studies is similar to the mean age of self-recognizers in the cross-sectional studies; toddlers begin to pass the MSR test reliability at about 18 months of age. For example, Nielsen, Dissanayake, and Kashima (2003) found that the mean, median, and mode of AOE were all 18 months. Courage et al. (2004) compared the emergence of MSR longitudinally in biweekly assessments as well as cross-sectionally. They found that, cross-sectionally, the mean age of self-recognizers was 20.27 months. When Courage et al. examined these data longitudinally by averaging the age at which each child first successfully passed the MSR task, the mean AOE was 17.1 months. When the authors examined the toddlers' stable MSR (i.e., when the toddlers passed several consecutive MSR tasks), the mean AOE was 19.3 months. Courage et al.'s data underscore the importance of longitudinal designs when examining the ontogeny of developmental attainments: The developmental trajectories in the cross-sectional samples showed a sharp increase from 30% of toddlers passing the MSR task at 16 months of age to 80% of toddlers passing the task at 17 months of age. The developmental trajectories in the longitudinal sample, however, showed a more gradual pattern of acquisition: Up to 40% of toddlers had passed the MSR task between 15 and 17 months of age, 50% had passed the task by the age of 17.5 and 18 months, 70% had passed the task by the age of 18.5 and 19 months, 80–90% had passed the task by the ages of 19.5 to 20.5 months, and 100% had passed the task by the ages of 21–23 months.

TODDLERS' EXPRESSIVE BEHAVIOR VIS-À-VIS THEIR SPECULAR IMAGE

In addition to mark-directed behavior, toddlers show a variety of behavioral patterns when observing their specular images (see also Amsterdam, 1972; Gallup, 1977; Priel & de Schonen, 1986). For example, toddlers playfully test the perfect contingency of their body movements and facial expressions with that of their specular images (experimenting). Since this behavior pattern indicates that toddlers are aware that it is their own image that the mirror reflects, it should be more prominent in self-recognizers (Bischof-Köhler, 1989; Dixon, 1957; Lewis & Brooks-Gunn, 1979; see also Povinelli, Rulf, Landau, & Bierschwale, 1993). In contrast, behavior patterns that indicate that toddlers do not realize that the mirror reflection is their own image (e.g., treating the specular image as a peer, looking behind the mirror, trying to get into the mirror) should occur more often in toddlers who do not recognize their specular images as themselves (Amsterdam, 1972; Bischof-Köhler, 1989).

The only study so far that has examined experimenting versus playmate behavior in relation to self-recognition status and in different sociocultural contexts found that both of these behaviors occurred more often in an autonomous sample (urban German) than in a relational (rural Nso in Cameroon) sample and were unrelated to MSR status (recognizer vs. nonrecognizer) (Keller, Kärtner, Borke, Yovsi, & Kleis, 2005). In the present study, we aimed to extend these findings by examining the association between mark-directed behavior (MSR) and other types of expressive mirror behavior (experimenting, playmate behavior, self- and other-referential pointing, etc.) and whether this association is moderated by toddlers' mirror familiarity or other specificities of different sociocultural contexts.

CULTURE-SPECIFIC DEVELOPMENTAL PATHWAYS

As shown in Table 1, most of the studies on MSR have been conducted on samples of toddlers from urban, highly educated, middle-class families from Western sociocultural contexts. Given that development is highly contingent upon sociocultural influences (Boesch, 2007; Greenfield, Keller, Fuligni, & Maynard, 2003; Henrich, Heine, & Norenzayan, 2010), the sociocultural specificity of these samples does not allow for generalizations beyond this very particular sociocultural context. There is ample evidence that the conception of the self and the self-in-relation-to-others differs markedly across sociocultural contexts (Kagitçibasi, 2007; Markus & Kitayama, 1991; Miller & Bersoff, 1998; Rothbaum, Pott, Azuma, Miyake, & Weisz, 2000). These cultural differences have important implications for development since the concept of a person—both self and other—is an integral component of a broader cultural model that has an interrelated system of norms, values, beliefs, and practices (Keller, 2007; Miller & Bersoff, 1992).

Cultural Models

Generally, cultural models are informed by the interplay of two basic human needs that are present in all individuals and all cultures: autonomy and relatedness (Kagitçibasi, 2007; Keller, 2007). These two dimensions are differentially emphasized in different cultural models, depending on various contextual factors associated with these cultural models. Specifically, in cultural models that prioritize autonomy, the decontextualized individual constitutes the basic social unit, whereas in cultural models that prioritize relatedness, the individual is defined in relation to others (Markus & Kitayama, 1991; Miller, 1987; Shweder & Bourne, 1982; Triandis, 1994). Cultural models oriented primarily toward autonomy stress the independence of the individual, personal freedom of choice, a contractual view of social relationships, and personal responsibility. Cultural models primarily oriented toward relatedness stress hierarchical social structures and duty-based role obligations and view interpersonal responsibilities as binding.

From a sociostructural perspective, we argue that the relative emphasis on autonomy and relatedness depends on social and structural aspects of environmental affordances and constraints (see also Kagitçibasi, 2007). For example, in subsistence-based farming ecologies, interdependencies among family members are a necessity and bring about prototypical relational norms and values such as obedience, respect, and responsibility (Nsamenang, 1992). In this way, both autonomy and relatedness are universal systems of beliefs and behavior that manifest to different degrees depending on the adaptive value that they have in a specific environment. On the macro-level, subsistence patterns, the economic system (e.g., subsistence-based ecology vs. cash economy), and the educational system are central environmental constituents of culture because they determine (at least in part) what constitutes everyday family life and socialization practices. On the micro-level, everyday family life and socialization practices within cultures are determined by family structure (nuclear or extended family), role allocation, everyday routines, the mother's age at the birth of her first child, and the number of siblings (LeVine et al., 1994; Whiting & Whiting, 1975). For example, prototypical autonomous cultural models focus on independence and individuality and are typically comprised of highly educated, urban, middle-class families in "Western" societies. Prototypical relational cultural models, on the other hand, focus on social hierarchy and social obligation and are typically comprised of rural families with basic levels of formal education living in subsistence-based "non-Western" ecologies (Keller, 2007).

Although the two prototypical cultural models of autonomy and relatedness constitute unambiguous and pure cultural models, there are also many hybrid cultural models. For example, highly educated, middle-class families in "non-Western" societies have been characterized as holding an autonomous-relational cultural model, that is, they emphasize both autonomy and relatedness in their everyday lives and in their child-rearing strategies. The high degree of formal education and specialized occupations foster autonomy, whereas traditional values and living in extended family systems strengthen duty-based interpersonal relationships (Kagitçibasi, 2007). It is important to note here that we do not equate culture with specific nations or countries; rather, there are specific sociodemographic contexts that should be associated with specific cultural models. Thus, it is not the nation or the society as a whole that forms individuals' cultural models but their specific social environments.

Culture and Development

Conceptions of the self and others—as constituent parts of the cultural models—are co-constructed during development by interactions with primary caretakers and by other socialization experiences (Greenfield et al., 2003;

Keller, 2007; Markus & Kitayama, 1991; Rothbaum et al., 2000). The basic assumption here is that cultural emphases, and hence socialization strategies, accelerate development of particular domains more than they do others, thereby constituting culture-specific developmental pathways. This assumption is generally referred to as the cultural precocity assumption (LeVine et al., 1994). In the domain of sociocognitive development, for example, there is evidence that developmental trajectories and achievements vary depending on cultural parenting practices and beliefs; specifically, there is support for culture-specific manifestations of the 2-month shift (Kärtner, Keller, & Yovsi, 2010), person perception (Miller, 1987), the development of morality (Miller & Bersoff, 1992, 1998), and false-belief understanding (Vinden, 1999, 2002; Wellman, Cross, & Watson, 2001) during childhood.

With regard to developmental achievements during the second year, studies have shown that toddlers have relative advances in specific developmental domains that lead to different developmental trajectories according to the cultural emphases of their caretakers. For example, in several rural, sub-Saharan sociocultural contexts that prioritize relatedness, proper demeanor and responsibility training are core socialization issues and caretakers have developed elaborate socialization practices intended to foster these competencies from early on (Keller, Yovsi, & Voelker, 2002; Ogunnaike & Houser, 2002). Accordingly, sub-Saharan toddlers comply more readily with maternal requests (Keller et al., 2004; Munroe & Munroe, 1975; Whiting & Whiting, 1975) than do toddlers in prototypical autonomous sociocultural contexts, in which early responsibility is deemed less important. In contrast, in autonomous sociocultural contexts, having children develop a sense of themselves as separate beings and an awareness of themselves as autonomous and independent agents (i.e., by making choices and articulating wishes and preferences) plays a key role in caretakers' socialization agenda (Keller, 2007; Keller et al., 2004; Markus & Kitayama, 1991; Rothbaum et al., 2000).

Culture and Self-Concept

Based on the above findings and the cultural precocity assumption, it seems likely that the dominant cultural model and associated socialization agendas should influence the development of MSR as an early indicator of toddlers' autonomous self-concept. The early development of a representation of the self as an autonomous agent who has subjective mental states should be fostered in sociocultural environments that prioritize autonomy (e.g., "Western," middle-class families) (Keller, 2007) and in autonomous-relational sociocultural environments (e.g., "non-Western," middle-class families) but not in prototypical relational sociocultural contexts (e.g., "non-Western," rural families) (Keller et al., 2004; Keller, Kärtner, et al., 2005).

One of the first studies on cross-cultural differences in the development of MSR seems, at first glance, to invalidate the idea that there are any sociocultural influences on early self-development. In their often-cited study, Priel and de Schonen (1986) compared groups of 6- to 12-, 13- to 19-, and 20- to 26-month-old toddlers from the Negev region in Israel who either came from urban middle-class or Bedouin-nomadic families. The authors describe a pattern of living and sleeping arrangements of Bedouin-nomadic families that is indicative of a prototypical relational sociocultural orientation. In contrast, the children from urban middle-class families came from families with autonomous or autonomous-relational orientations. It is important to note, however, that Priel and de Schonen did not set out to directly examine sociocultural effects on MSR performance. Rather, they examined the effect of mirror experience on toddlers' MSR performance; the Bedouin-nomadic children had no experience with mirrors or reflective surfaces whereas the urban children did have ample mirror experience. Despite this difference in mirror experience, however, Priel and de Schonen found that the frequency of mark-directed behavior did not differ between the two samples. This result is puzzling; the Bedouin-nomadic children's lack of mirror experience teamed with their relational sociocultural orientation should, if anything, have amplified the difference in mark-directed behavior between the mirror-experienced (and autonomy-supporting) and nonexperienced groups. If we examine the data more closely, however, the authors report that 17.5% of all 13- to 19-month-olds and 15% of mirror-experienced 13- to 19-month-olds displayed mark-directed behavior. As discussed previously, by the age of 18–20 months, 40–65% of children display mark-directed behavior on MSR tasks and recognition rates are below 35% for toddlers younger than 18 months (see Table 1). The authors did not, however, compare the mean ages of recognizers between the two groups nor did they specify the exact distribution of ages within each age group. Given that the age ranges were very wide (6 months per age group), the authors' rather coarse-grained analysis may have missed subtle developmental differences between the two different groups of toddlers. It is also noteworthy that no study, to date, has replicated Priel & de Schonen's (1986) findings.

In contrast to Priel and de Schonen's (1986) findings, there are at least three other studies that have provided support for the cultural precocity assumption regarding self-development and self-other differentiation. In a longitudinal study, Keller et al. (2004) found that a higher percentage of 19-month-old toddlers from an autonomous context (Athens, Greece: 68%) or an autonomous-relational context (San Jose, Costa Rica: 50%) passed the MSR test than did same-aged toddlers from a relational sociocultural context (rural Nso, Cameroon: 3%). Keller et al. suggested that early socialization experiences (e.g., amount of face-to-face contact and object stimulation) provided a possible explanation for these cultural differences. These early socialization experiences followed the same pattern on the cultural level: The more face-to-face contact and object stimulation the children experienced during mother–infant interaction at 3 months of age on average in a specific sociocultural context, the higher the percentage of toddlers who recognized themselves in a mirror at 19 months of age.

In another longitudinal study, Keller, Kärtner, et al. (2005) found that 73% of toddlers from autonomy-oriented urban German families and only 15% of toddlers from relatedness-oriented rural Cameroonian Nso families recognized themselves in a mirror at 19 months of age. Whether toddlers recognized themselves or not was related to the number of contingent responses they experienced in response to their communicative signals during mother–infant interaction when they were 3 months old. Thus, it seems as if MSR emerges earlier in those sociocultural contexts in which infants' autonomy is emphasized (i.e., urban middle-class families in "Western" societies) and that this effect is mediated by sociocultural differences in the caretakers' normative orientations and early caretaker–infant interaction. In support of this assumption, Broesch, Callaghan, Henrich, Murphy, and Rochat (2010) found considerably later onsets of MSR in different relational sociocultural contexts.

Although the studies on MSR development by Keller et al. (2004) and Keller, Kärtner, et al. (2005) provide the first empirical evidence in support of the cultural precocity assumption, there are at least three other alternative explanations for the sociocultural differences noted in these two studies. First, the low rates of MSR in the Cameroonian Nso samples in both studies could be explained by the low degree of mirror familiarity in the rural Nso culture, where mirrors are much less common. Given these findings (and in contrast to Priel and de Schonen's [1986] findings), mirror familiarity should be reconsidered as a potential explanation for low recognition rates of toddlers from relational contexts. Second, since both studies used rural Nso samples to reflect a prototypical relational sociocultural context, it could be argued that idiosyncrasies of the Nso sample (e.g., culture-specific norms of expressive behavior) led to the low rates of MSR rather than a systematic difference in the sample's sociocultural orientation. Finally, it is possible that the mark-and-mirror task measures different constructs between the sociocultural samples (Broesch et al., 2010). In this way, is it an appropriate and valid task for relational sociocultural contexts?

THE PRESENT STUDY

The central hypothesis of the present study is that toddlers' sense of themselves as autonomous agents who have subjective mental states (as measured by MSR performance) will develop earlier in sociocultural contexts in which caretakers emphasize autonomous socialization goals. There are three ways in which this study is distinct from earlier cross-cultural studies on MSR and, thus, contributes to the existing literature. First, previous studies have often used one-point-in-time approaches by examining the percentage of toddlers who recognized themselves in a mirror at a specific age (usually 18 months). This method does not give a true indication of age of onset and the developmental trajectories of MSR. Therefore, in the present study, we used a cross-sequential design that combined longitudinal and cross-sectional features. Groups of toddlers from four different sociocultural contexts (urban German, urban Indian, rural Indian, rural Nso) fell into one of six age cohorts at their first assessment (16, 17, 18, 19, 20, or 21 months), and their developmental trajectories of MSR were traced weekly for a period of 6 weeks. In this way, the present study provides further insight into the developmental trajectories of MSR between the ages of 16 and 22.25 months in different sociocultural contexts. Second, we analyzed the development of MSR in different prototypical relational sociocultural contexts. When we first embarked on this study, both of the previous studies that had reported cross-cultural differences in MSR were based on comparisons with rural Nso samples (Keller et al., 2004; Keller, Kärtner, et al., 2005). To exclude idiosyncrasies of this specific sociocultural context that may have led to these cross-cultural differences, we included a second prototypical relational sociocultural context: The rural Indian sample. Third, one of the main aims of the present study was to systematically establish the cross-cultural validity of MSR. In order to do so, we first tested the validity of MSR by selecting an external criterion (pronoun usage) with which it should be correlated. Second, we have also attempted to systematically rule out potential alternative explanations for cross-cultural differences in MSR. These factors include familiarity with mirrors, culture-specific norms of expressive behavior, and differences in motivation to tactually explore a novel mark.

Sociocultural Sample Selection

The guiding principle for the selection of sociocultural contexts was that there should be samples from different sociocultural contexts that emphasize autonomy to different degrees. We recruited two samples that emphasized autonomy: A sample from a prototypical autonomous sociocultural context that prioritizes autonomy (urban German) and a sample from an autonomous-relational context that emphasizes autonomy and relatedness to similar degrees (urban Indian). In addition, we recruited more than one sample from prototypical relational sociocultural contexts (rural Indian, rural Nso) in order to exclude sample idiosyncrasies as a potential explanation for differences in MSR. Ideally, one of the relational (i.e., rural Indian) and the autonomous-relational (i.e., urban Indian) sociocultural contexts should differ only in those parameters that are constitutive of their cultural model (e.g., SES, education, household size), whereas all other parameters should be comparable (e.g., nationality, language, religion).

Urban German Middle-Class Families

The urban German middle-class sample was recruited in Osnabrück, a medium-sized city of 180,000 inhabitants in lower Saxony, a federal state in northwest Germany. The parents in our sample had medium to high levels of formal education and had typical middle-class occupations, for example, teachers, engineers, or businessmen. In middle-class Germany, the nuclear family is the dominant family type. Infants spend most of their time at home with their mothers during the first year. From the age of 3 years, most children go to kindergarten. The role distribution in most German families is still traditional in that it is mostly mothers who take care of the infants while the fathers are at work (Keller, Zach, & Abels, 2005; Keller, 2006).

German middle-class mothers socialize their children toward individuality, autonomy (Keller, 2007), and self-reliance (LeVine & Norman, 2001). These mothers value exclusive dyadic interaction and believe that children need to spend time on their own in order to become more independent (Keller et al., 2004; Keller, Voelker, & Yovsi, 2005). In this way, German middle-class families should have a predominantly autonomous sociocultural orientation.

Urban Indian Middle-Class Families

The urban Indian middle-class sample was recruited in the Delhi area (the National Capital Region consisting of New Delhi and surrounding satellite cities). The parents in our sample were all Hindus, held medium to high levels of formal education, and had typical middle-class occupations, for example, businessmen, service, and education. Typically, Delhi middle-class households are composed of the nuclear family plus additional members of the older generations and other relatives who stay with the family. Often, mothers work outside of the home and hired domestic helpers assist with the care of children and household work. Children in these families are cared for primarily by their parents and have easy access to material and nonmaterial resources. In comparison to the rural Indian families (see below), there is far less interaction between neighbors and doors of homes are usually closed with limited free access. Facilities for outdoor play differ from neighborhood to neighborhood and older children usually play within or around their own homes or in nearby parks if these are available (outside play is nevertheless restricted and supervised). All homes have some appliances for housework and civic amenities are available. Markets are abundant and are nearby to most homes. The city is well equipped with good transport, health care, education, recreation, and law and order facilities.

Indian middle-class families place a great deal of emphasis on social relationships and interpersonal responsibilities (Chaudhary, 2004; Miller & Bersoff, 1992; Miller, Bersoff, & Harwood, 1990; Miller & Luthar, 1989; Wang & Chaudhary, 2005). In a number of cross-cultural studies, Miller and her colleagues (Miller et al., 1990; Miller & Luthar, 1989) have shown that Hindu Indians view interpersonal relations and helping others in fully moral terms; there is both a sense of objective obligation and a sense of being within the scope of legitimate regulation. Miller and Bersoff (1992) have also shown that from 8 years of age, the majority of Hindu Indians give priority to interpersonal responsibilities relative to considerations of justice. The authors argue that this differential emphasis is due to an intrinsic and obligatory perspective on relationships that is stressed in Hindu Indian culture as compared to the more voluntaristic view of social relationships that is stressed in Euro-American culture. At the same time, however, Indian middle-class families place much more emphasis on autonomy than do lower class Indian families because they are highly educated and their occupations require flexibility and self-determination (Raman, 2003; Sinha & Tripathi, 1994; Verma & Saraswathi, 2002). Thus, children are encouraged to be independent and assertive as well as respectful and sensitive to others. In this way, Indian urban middle-class families should have an autonomous-relational sociocultural orientation in which both autonomy and relatedness hold similar degrees of importance (see Kağıtçıbaşı, 2007). In other words, these families should emphasize autonomy as much as the German families, but they should also emphasize relational socialization goals to the same degree as autonomous socialization goals (Kagitçibasi, 2007; Kärtner, 2008; Keller, 2007).

Rural Indian Families

The rural Indian sample was recruited from three villages in rural Rajasthan (Neemrana), Uttar Pradesh (Reelkha), and Haryana (near Karnal city). The three villages are located between 90 km North and 120 km East of Delhi. All three villages have many similar features and are typical of northern Indian villages. The parents in our sample were mainly Hindus and most adults had only basic levels of formal education. The majority of villagers have agricultural jobs, although some also work in the trade, driving, craftwork, and daily-wage-earning industries. There seems to be clear division in the work done by men and women. Whereas men take on tasks that are intense and seasonal (e.g., agricultural, outdoors work), the women organize the home. Women are typically not employed outside of the home except if they are teachers in a local school or if they are health care personnel. At home, women care for the cattle, tend to the crop fields, and complete the housework (without the use of household appliances that are common in urban homes). Family wealth consists of farms, land property, and number of cattle, and is usually shared by all family members.

Typically, these rural areas have many concrete homes and other, more temporary, structures made of adobe. The main village is a cluster of homes with some central spaces (e.g., local government center, school) and fields for agriculture surround the village. Within the village, the streets meander between the houses and are mostly unpaved, which makes them difficult to negotiate during the rainy season. Electricity and running water (community taps) are available for most of the larger homes, but are not as readily available for the poorer areas of the village. In general, the water supply is timed at regular intervals and the electricity supply is intermittent. There are some small stores amid the houses that sell essential goods. For most of the larger purchases, villagers depend on the nearby markets. Connectivity in terms of transportation to nearby towns and cities is ad hoc and intermittent, relying mostly on private taxis. Most of the houses are reasonably spacious and are designed such that the rooms surround a central open space. Some homes also have a room for cattle at the entrance. Clusters of two or three villages have one common post office. As far as telecommunications is concerned, there is no Internet access in villages and very few of the houses have direct phone lines. With regard to educational facilities, each of the three villages has a primary school and a middle school (up to Grade 5 or 10). There is also a preschool program provided by the government. The facilities for children's education are sparse, however; there are many challenges such as infrequent teaching, poor classroom and bathroom facilities, and inadequate teaching and learning materials.

The patriarchal, joint family system is predominant in these rural areas; there is a common kitchen and many family members reside in the same house or in adjacent homes. Usually each household has many generations living together, thus, the concept of "multiple parenting" is clearly reflected in day-to-day life. All family members are usually involved in childcare, but women are considered to be the primary caretakers. Daily activities such as feeding, bathing, putting to sleep, and care throughout the day are commonly shared by the older women. Male family members usually indulge children by taking them to places outside of the home. Children usually play with improvised toys made of natural materials that they find around the home and in the fields. The social boundaries between families are very flexible and villagers walk freely in and out of each others' homes. Toddlers' activities are mostly unsupervised although adults are always present in the area. By the time children are 5 or 6 (sometimes earlier in cases of children being cared for by older siblings), they roam freely in the village.

With regard to socialization patterns, rural Indian families exert absolute moral authority over their children (Kakar, 1981; Lannoy, 1971; Sarangapani, 1999). The main socialization goals within families are obedience to the parents, compliance, dutifulness, and respect for older members of the family (Abels et al., 2005; Chaudhary, 2004; Kakar, 1981). In this way, rural Indian Hindu families should have a predominantly relational sociocultural orientation.

Rural Nso Families

The Nso sample was recruited from small villages scattered on the hills around Kumbo, a city of about 120,000 inhabitants in the Bui Division of the Northwest Province of Cameroon. The Nso are one of the largest ethnic groups in the Western grass fields and Kumbo (with its palace and traditional king) is the capital and the cultural center of the Nsoland. In the villages, most adults have little formal education and mainly work in agriculture, although some also work in the trade, driving, craftwork, and daily-wage-earning industries. Most Nso villagers live on subsistence-based farming and the whole family, including children, helps with this (Yovsi, 2003).

Nso villages are made up of several compounds, in which houses are grouped around a central, open yard. Unpaved roads or little paths connect separate compounds; these roads become difficult to negotiate during the rainy season. Agricultural fields surround the compounds. Houses are usually constructed from red adobe bricks and windows are made from planks or bamboo. Wealthier houses are built from concrete blocks and have cement floors and ribbed roofs. The kitchen is a separate building and consists of a fire pit and shelves to store food and utensils. Electricity and running water (aside from community taps) are available for some of the larger homes, but are rather uncommon. As far as telecommunications is concerned, there is no Internet access in villages and only very few of the houses (and schools) have direct phone lines. Some families do, however, have mobile phones and slow Internet access is available in Kumbo. Villagers depend on the market that is held in Kumbo once a week for selling or purchasing goods. Connectivity in terms of transportation to nearby cities is ad hoc and intermittent, relying mostly on private taxis. Basic education is mandatory and there are several public and denominational nursery and primary schools. Most children attend school up to elementary level (Grade 7). Secondary schools are only to be found in Kumbo. There are health centers in the villages but they lack infrastructure and most villagers prefer traditional medicine.

The settlement pattern is patrilocal and every male owns land within the lineage territory where he builds and settles with his family, usually adjacent to his father's or grandfather's compound. Men achieve high social status through *keng* (wealth) in the form of raffia palms, coffee plantations, forests, and houses. The rural Nso have an extended family system of three or more generations. Similar to the rural Indian setting, there is a clear division of labor: While men take on intense and representative tasks, women organize the home. Families share everyday activities, including childcare. Thus, children are socialized in a dense social network including parents, siblings, relatives, grandparents, and neighbors. Childcare is a communal responsibility; after the birth of a child, everybody in the community has an obligation toward his or her care and social development (Nsamenang, 1992; Yovsi, 2003). Similar to the rural Indian setting, Nso parents demand complete obedience to parents and older members of the family; unfaltering conformity is children's primary duty (Keller, 2007; Nsamenang, 1992). Compliance and dutifulness from early on are explicit instructions for socialization (Ogunnaike & Houser, 2002). In this way, rural Nso farming families should have a predominantly relational sociocultural orientation.

Testing Alternative Explanations of MSR

In addition to cross-cultural differences in caretakers' normative orientations and parenting behavior, there are a number of other influences on MSR that differ systematically across sociocultural contexts. There are three alternative explanations for the cross-cultural differences observed in MSR rates: (1) Familiarity with mirrors, (2) culture-specific norms of expressive behavior, and (3) differences in the motivation to tactually explore a novel mark. For each of these alternative explanations, we will outline the precautions we took to estimate the degree to which the respective variables might influence the toddlers' behavior.

Familiarity With Mirrors

Comparing urban middle-class families from "Western" cultures to rural families with a basic level of formal education from "non-Western" cultures necessarily conflates differences in the cultures' socialization agendas with differences in mirror familiarity. In urban, middle-class environments, toddlers see and have seen themselves in mirrors very often and mirrors are a part of everyday life both at home and in public. In rural, subsistence-based environments, however, possessing a mirror is not common and toddlers rarely see themselves in a mirror or any other reflective surface, even in public places. The cross-sequential design that we have used in the present study facilitates quantification of the effect of mirror familiarity: If familiarity with mirrors does affect the capacity for MSR, there should be a significant interaction between culture (urban vs. rural) and week of assessment. Specifically, the self-recognition rates of toddlers from rural contexts (e.g., rural Cameroon and rural India), who have no previous mirror experience but who develop increasing familiarity with mirrors, should increase at a faster rate than should the recognition rates of toddlers from urban contexts (e.g., Germany and urban India). In this way, any differences in self-recognition rates across successive weeks in the urban samples can be solely attributed to developmental processes. In contrast, differences in self-recognition rates across successive weeks in the rural samples can be attributed to developmental processes *plus* increasing mirror familiarity.

Norms of Expressive Behavior

Keller, Kärtner, et al. (2005) suggested that culture-specific norms of expressive behavior may explain the reduced rates of self-recognizers in prototypical relational sociocultural contexts. It is possible that previous studies of MSR underestimated the rate of self-recognizers in rural settings due to culture-specific, reduced rates of expressive behavior in general. Any operational definition of MSR necessarily includes behavioral criteria. Therefore, in sociocultural contexts in which expressiveness is deemed undesirable or in which the goal of socialization is to raise a calm, emotionally balanced, unexpressive child—as is the case for rural Nso mothers (Keller & Otto, 2009)— MSR may be an inadequate and invalid tool to measure self-recognition. In fact, Broesch et al. (2010) have suggested that what appears to be a delay in the age of onset (AOE) of self-recognition in some cultural contexts may be due to strong cultural emphases on obedience, compliance, and behavioral inhibition.

In order to determine whether culture-specific norms of expressive behavior play a role in the reduced rates of self-recognition in relational sociocultural contexts, we examined children's participation in a number of other expressive behaviors during the MSR task (e.g., treating the image as a playmate, experimenting, and self- and other-referential pointing). If culture-specific norms of expressive behavior do affect MSR performance, then these differences should not be specific to mark-directed behavior during the test. Rather, there should be systematic differences in any type of behavior shown during the mark-and-mirror test.

Motivation for Tactile Exploration

Related to the idea of culture-specific norms of expressive behavior is toddlers' motivation to touch the mark on their face. It is possible that some toddlers do recognize the novel mark on their face but are just not motivated to touch it. This motivation could differ systematically between different sociocultural contexts, yielding cross-cultural differences in MSR. There is some evidence that motivation for tactile exploration does not contribute to unsuccessful MSR performance, however; Nielsen and Dissanayke (2004) placed a sticker on the backs of infants' hands (in addition to a sticker on the forehead) to ensure that failure on the MSR task was not due to a lack of motivation to retrieve the sticker. They found that all but one nonrecognizer removed the sticker from their hand—these infants were clearly motivated but still showed no MSR.

In order to determine whether motivation plays a role in MSR performance, we assessed whether rural toddlers were generally less motivated to tactually explore a novel mark. To do this, we measured: (1) Toddlers' reactions to a novel mark on the face of a familiar person (marked-mother task) and (2) toddlers' reactions to a mark placed surreptitiously on the back of their own hand (marked-hand task). If toddlers are simply not motivated to touch the mark on their face, these toddlers should also not touch a novel mark in either the marked-mother task or in the marked-hand task. We tested this hypothesis both on the individual level and on the sample level.

Given all of these potential influences, we tested the cross-cultural validity of MSR as an index of the toddlers' sense of themselves (and others) as autonomous agents by analyzing age trends, the stability of MSR across weeks, and the correlation with pronoun usage in each cultural context. Furthermore, we micro-analyzed specific behavior patterns shown in front of the mirror, for example, toddlers' gaze, experimenting, playmate, and pointing behavior.

Summary and Hypotheses

In the present study, we examined the development of MSR in four sociocultural contexts that hold prototypical autonomous (urban German middle-class) or prototypical relational (rural India, rural Nso) sociocultural models or that emphasize both autonomy and relatedness to similar degrees (urban Indian middle-class). Based on a cross-sequential study design, we plotted a detailed developmental course of MSR for the critical age span of 16–22.25 months of age. This study provides the first empirical examination of the cross-cultural reliability and validity of the MSR test as an indicator of an autonomous self-concept.

There were four main hypotheses. First, the general shape of the developmental course of self-recognition should be similar in all of the samples (i.e., rates of successful MSR should increase with age). Second, toddlers from urban sociocultural environments that emphasize autonomous socialization goals should recognize themselves earlier than should toddlers from rural sociocultural contexts that emphasize relational socialization goals. The developmental course of self-recognition should not differ between the two autonomy-supporting sociocultural contexts (urban German and urban

Indian) or between the two relational sociocultural contexts (rural Indian and rural Nso). Third, MSR performance should be correlated with pronoun usage, thus supporting the cross-cultural validity of MSR as an indicator of an autonomous self-concept. Finally, if sociocultural differences in MSR performance do reflect sociocultural differences in the emergence of an autonomous self-concept, then MSR performance should not differ as a function of culture-specific differences in mirror familiarity, norms of expressive behavior, or motivation for tactile exploration.

METHOD

DESIGN

In the present study, we traced the developmental trajectories of MSR of toddlers from different age cohorts (16, 17, 18, 19, 20, or 21 months ±2 days at first assessment) using weekly (±2 days) assessments for a period of 6 weeks. This unique design, in which adjacent cohorts overlapped, enabled us to examine effects of mirror familiarity on MSR performance; there were same-aged cohorts who were at different stages of the assessment process and, therefore, had differing degrees of mirror and task familiarity. For example, toddlers who were aged 16 months at their first assessment were the same age at their fifth assessment (17 months) as were toddlers who were aged 17 months at their first assessment but they had a greater degree of mirror and task familiarity. Based on earlier studies, we focused on the critical age span for MSR in each of the four sociocultural contexts. Because the critical age span for MSR differs as a function of sociocultural context, not all age cohorts were assessed in all four sociocultural contexts. Given that most studies on the development of MSR in autonomous contexts report that 50% of toddlers pass the MSR task at about 18 months of age and most toddlers pass the task by the age of 21 months (e.g., Nielsen et al., 2003, 2006), we recruited four age-cohorts of 16-, 17-, 18-, and 19-month olds in the urban German sociocultural context and three age-cohorts of 17-, 18-, and 19-month olds in the urban Indian context. Research has shown that children from relational contexts begin to pass the MSR task consistently at a later age than do children from autonomy-oriented contexts (Broesch et al., 2010; Keller et al., 2004; Keller, Kärtner et al., 2005). Therefore, we recruited three age-cohorts of 18-, 19-, and 20-month olds in the rural Indian sociocultural context and four age-cohorts of 18-, 19-, 20-, and 21-month olds in the rural Nso sociocultural context. In this way, there were cohorts of 18- and 19-month-olds in all four sociocultural contexts and additional cohorts of younger toddlers in the autonomy-supporting contexts and additional cohorts of older toddlers in the relational sociocultural contexts.

In addition to the MSR task, we administered the marked-mother task at the second and sixth assessments in all age-cohorts and samples, and the marked-hand task at the third and fourth assessments in all of the rural Indian and part of the rural Nso (20- and 21-month old cohorts) sample. Furthermore, we administered questionnaires regarding relevant sociodemographic and other background information at the first assessment and questionnaires regarding caretakers' socialization goals at the second assessment for all cohorts and all samples.

SOCIOCULTURAL SAMPLES

The recruitment of participants in each of the sociocultural contexts followed local customs.

Urban German Middle-Class Families

Participants were recruited through announcements in mother–child classes, in the local newspaper, and on the local radio station. Parents held medium to high levels of formal education and had typical middle-class occupations, for example, teachers, engineers, or businessmen. Mothers were either Catholic (39%), Protestant (44%), or had no religious affiliation (17%).

Urban Indian Middle-Class Families

Participants were recruited primarily through well-known persons with high social regard, for example, local medical doctors. In order for the Delhi families to feel that they could trust the research team, they were invited to call the researchers for more specific information about the study. Other participants in the Delhi sample were recruited by word-of-mouth through acquaintances whose toddlers were already enrolled in the study. All families were Hindu, and parents held medium to high levels of formal education and had typical middle-class occupations, for example, businessmen, service, and education.

Rural Indian Families

With regard to sample recruitment, we located villages in which relatives of the Delhi research assistants lived. This recruitment method was critical, because otherwise the research team was likely to be mistaken for local government or health-care officials who villagers usually distrust. Once entry was made into the village, the researchers became known as visitors to the particular home (of the relatives) and gradually families with children of the required ages were located through house-to-house visits. All families were Hindu and most parents had little formal education. The majority of parents had agricultural jobs, although some parents also worked in the trade, driving, craftwork, and daily-wage-earning industries.

Rural Nso Families

With regard to sample recruitment, we made personal contact with people who held official positions with respect to community life. We were fortunate in that one of the authors of the present study is an Nso and grew up in the area. Her father is one of the seven notables (*shufai*) in the traditional ruler system, which is led by the traditional king (*fon*). Potential participants were identified by the health center that keeps birth records. These families were then contacted by local research assistants after the lineage heads approved participation. Interested mothers participated if their family heads consented. All families were Catholic with a strong background in animistic tradition. Most parents had little formal education and mainly worked in agriculture, although some parents also worked in the trade, driving, craftwork, and daily-wage-earning industries.

PARTICIPANTS

There were 276 families that participated in the present study (urban German = 82, urban Indian = 60, rural Indian = 54, rural Nso = 80). Children were aged 16, 17, 18, 19, 20, or 21 months (±2 days) at the first MSR assessment. There were 17–23 toddlers in each age group in each of the sociocultural contexts (see Table 2).

TABLE 2
NUMBER OF PARTICIPANTS IN EACH SOCIOCULTURAL CONTEXT AND AGE COHORT

	Age Cohort (Months)						
	16	17	18	19	20	21	Total
Urban German	22	20	20	20			82
Urban Indian		20	20	20			60
Rural Indian			19	18	17		54
Rural Nso			23	17	20	20	80
Total	22	40	82	75	37	20	276

METHOD

With regard to sociodemographic variables, gender was equally distributed across samples; on average, 51% of all children were girls (range = 48% in rural India to 55% in rural Nso). There were significantly less firstborn children in the rural Nso sample (35%) than there were in all other samples (urban Germany = 57%, urban India = 54%, rural India = 53%), $\chi^2 = 9.37$, $p < .05$. Of the remaining toddlers, most had one or two siblings (urban Germany = 40%, urban India = 46%, rural India = 41%, rural Nso = 38%), some had three or four siblings (urban Germany = 3%, urban India = 0%, rural India = 6%, rural Nso = 16%), and 11% of the rural Nso sample had five or more siblings. There were more people living in the same household in the urban Indian, rural Indian, and rural Nso samples than there were in the urban German sample (see Table 3). The dominant family type in the urban German sample was the nuclear family (93%), whereas the extended family was the dominant family type in the two Indian samples (urban = 74%, rural = 84%). There were less extended family members living in the same household in the rural Nso sample (44%). The patrilocal settlement pattern of the Nso implies, however, that, in most cases, the extended family lives literally next door. Mothers from the autonomy-supporting sociocultural contexts (urban German and urban Indian) were significantly older than were mothers from the relational sociocultural contexts (rural Indian and rural Nso). They also held higher educational attainments than did mothers from the relational sociocultural contexts (see Table 3).

PROCEDURE

At the first point of contact (by telephone in the urban samples and by a home visit in the rural samples), a research assistant and the mother agreed upon a weekday and a time that was suitable for the research assistant to visit for the next 6 weeks. Setting appointment times for data collection in the rural samples was less straightforward as the women's days are so tightly packed. Schedules in villages are highly dependent upon the changing daily domestic, familial, and agricultural requirements of the families. In total, there were 1,576 family visits and MSR assessments. Overall, 79% of the toddlers participated in all six MSR assessments (urban German = 74%, urban Indian = 93%, rural Indian = 69%, rural Nso = 79%). Due to illness, holidays, or sudden impediments, 16% participated in five out of the six assessments (urban German = 21%, urban Indian = 7%, rural Indian = 20%, rural Nso = 15%) and only 5% participated in four out of the six assessments (urban German = 5%, urban Indian = 0%, rural Indian = 11%, rural Nso = 6%), $\chi^2 = 14.27$, $p < .05$.

All families were visited at home by two local research assistants. At the beginning of the first visit, one of the assistants explained the project and the

TABLE 3

SOCIODEMOGRAPHIC INFORMATION AS A FUNCTION OF SOCIOCULTURAL CONTEXT

	Sociocultural Sample					
	Urban German	Urban Indian	Rural Indian	Rural Nso	$F_{(df)}/\chi^2$	η_p^2
No. of people living in household	3.66 (.91)[a]	6.20 (1.71)[b]	8.67 (4.56)[c]	6.13 (2.36)[b]	$F_{(3, 250)} = 40.71$***	.33
No. of cohabiting siblings	.55 (.79)[a]	.57 (.59)[a]	.71 (.98)[a]	1.73 (1.86)[b]	$F_{(3, 238)} = 14.78$***	.16
Maternal age (years)	34.01 (4.41)[a]	31.21 (5.61)[a]	23.94 (4.40)[b]	28.26 (7.76)[c]	$F_{(3, 252)} = 34.34$***	.29
Maternal education (years)	14.39 (3.36)[a]	17.00 (1.35)[a]	6.64 (4.84)[b]	7.54 (2.11)[b]	$F_{(3, 247)} = 153.12$***	.65
Extended family living in household (%)	7.3	73.8	84.2	43.8	$\chi^2 = 85.23$***	
At least one cohabiting grandparent (%)	6.1	71.4	81.6	33.8	$\chi^2 = 86.12$***	
At least one cohabiting great grandparent (%)	0.0	9.5	15.8	0.0	$\chi^2 = 23.10$***	

Note. Standard deviations are in parentheses. Superscripts of different letters indicate significant differences ($p < .05$) between the respective sociocultural samples (based on simple main effects testing with Bonferroni adjustment for averages and χ^2 tests for percentages). η_p^2 = partial eta-squared. There were reduced sample sizes for urban and rural Indian samples because it was not possible to obtain questionnaire data from all families.

*** $p < .001$.

type of assessments to the mother while the other assistant played with the child and established rapport. Apart from exceptional cases, the same two research assistants administered the MSR task each week, the marked-mother task in the second and sixth weeks, and the marked-hand task in the third and fourth weeks. The research assistants also administered questionnaires to the mothers that assessed relevant sociodemographic and other background information (week 1) and caretakers' socialization goals (week 2). In the following sections, we describe the procedure and coding of each of these assessments.

Questionnaires

After the research assistants had administered the MSR task, mothers answered questionnaires regarding relevant background information (week 1) and the importance of various socialization goals (week 2).

Background Information

Relevant background information included general sociodemographic data such as the parents' education and occupations. There were also two yes/no questions regarding: (a) the child's pronoun use (i.e., "Has your child ever said 'I', 'Mine,' 'self/ me,' or similar words?") and (b) the child's usage of his/her own name (i.e., "Has your child ever said his own name?"). Toddlers were assigned a score of 1 if their mothers answered "yes" on one or both of these questions. Toddlers were assigned a score of 0 if their mothers answered "no" to both questions. While the urban German and urban Indian mothers filled out the questionnaires themselves, the questions and possible answers were read aloud to the rural Indian and rural Nso mothers and respective answers were ticked by the assistant. The questionnaires were administered in this way because filling out questionnaires is a very unusual activity in prototypical relational sociocultural contexts.

Socialization Goals

Because giving graded responses on Likert scales is highly unusual in both of the rural settings, we assessed mothers' socialization goals using a pairwise comparison procedure based on two sets of four items. One set of items described autonomy-oriented socialization goals (e.g., developing personal talents and interests, learning to express own preferences very clearly) while the other set of items described relatedness-oriented socialization goals (e.g., learning to do what parents say, learning to share with others). Each of the eight items was compared with each of the other seven items, one at a time, constituting a total of 28 pairwise comparisons. The order of autonomous and relatedness-oriented goals was counterbalanced across pairs. For each pair, mothers were asked to indicate which of the two goals was more important to them (or whether they were of equal importance) regarding the development of their child. In terms of scoring, a preference for one goal over another was scored as $+1$ for the preferred goal and -1 for the nonpreferred goal (e.g., preference for goal A over goal B was scored as $+1$ for goal A and -1 for goal B). If two goals were rated as equally important, they each received a score of 0 (no difference). Using this procedure, we were able to measure not only the relative importance of each of the goals but also the degree to which one goal is more important than another. More importantly, response sets (i.e., respondents who give generally high or low responses on Likert-scaled items) are mostly precluded by this approach because all respondents have the same mean across items (i.e., 0). Thus, it is easier to compare and interpret the relative importance of each goal across respondents without any statistical adjustment.

Mirror Assessments

At all four research sites, mirrors were of comparable size (width = 55–65 cm, height = 100–125 cm) and children could see their full figures in the mirror. The mirror was either fixed on a pressboard or set into a wooden frame. The assessments with the urban German and urban Indian children took place inside, usually in the family's living room or in the child's room. The assessments with the rural Indian and rural Nso children usually took place outside the house, which is reflective of daily routines in family life. Moreover, lighting conditions inside the houses were poor and did not allow for filming. In the following sections we describe the procedures used in the MSR and mirror behavior observation assessments. Each assessment was video recorded by one of the research assistants.

MSR Assessments

During each of the assessments, mothers were asked to stay nearby. All other people present during testing were instructed to keep out of the area reflected by the mirror either by sitting next to or behind the mirror or by leaving the area. Everyone present was instructed to keep quiet and not to say anything to the child that might help him or her to localize the mark. When the family felt comfortable with the visitors and the procedure, one research assistant set up the covered mirror in a suitable place, usually leaning against a wall with no direct source of reflective light. After everything was set up, the research assistant tried to attract the child's interest in the mirror by uncovering the mirror together with the child.

The MSR task consisted of two phases. In the first phase, the unmarked children stayed in front of the mirror. If children lost interest or left, the research assistant or the mothers tried to redirect their attention by calling them back or putting a toy close to the mirror. This phase lasted, depending on the toddlers' interest in the mirror, 10–15 min in the first and fifth assessments and 5 min in all other assessments. In the second phase, a mark was surreptitiously applied on the toddler's face and their subsequent reaction to their mirror image was observed. To apply the mark on the child's face, the research assistant put some odorless, hypoallergenic lipstick on the mother's (German sample) or her own (all other samples) finger unbeknownst to the child. Research assistants used red lipstick to mark the faces of the German and Indian children and white lipstick to mark the faces of the Nso children. In the German sample, mothers put the mark on their toddlers' faces because a pilot study revealed that mothers thought it was intrusive if research assistants touched their children. By pretending to blow the child's nose or clean the child's face, the mother or the research assistant put the mark on the child's face after having led the child away from the mirror. In most cases, the mark was placed close to the nose (on one side). In all cases the mark was placed surreptitiously and in a way that it could not be seen directly (e.g., through peripheral vision). In the second phase of the rouge test, the toddler was led back to the mirror and again looked at his or her mirror image for 5 min (or shorter if he or she displayed clear mark-directed behavior).

Other Mirror Behavior

During each of the MSR assessments, we also observed other aspects of the toddlers' behavior in front of the mirror, namely the toddlers' looking, experimenting, playmate, and pointing behavior. Looking behavior was defined as looking at the mirror and, more specifically, looking at one's specular image. Experimenting behavior was defined as episodes in which toddlers experimented with their mirror image by moving their face, their head, or their body slower, faster, or more abruptly while keenly observing their specular image. Playmate behavior was defined as episodes in which toddlers treated their specular image as a peer, such as by greeting the specular image or offering an object (e.g., toy) to the specular image. Pointing behavior was defined as a pointing gesture either pointing at the specular image (i.e., self-referential pointing) or at somebody or something else (i.e., other-referential pointing).

Marked-Mother Assessments

In all of the samples, we administered the marked-mother task in the second and sixth assessments to see whether toddlers would refer to a novel mark on their mother's face. After the MSR task had been administered, the mirror was covered and the mother marked her face (usually close to the nose) while the experimenter distracted the toddler. The mother then turned toward her toddler and played with him/her for 5 min as if nothing had changed (or shorter if the child showed clear signs of mark-directed behavior). If the child did not look at his/her mother, the mother drew the child's attention by calling his/her name. In total, 28 marked-mother assessments were excluded because toddlers did not look at their mothers or only once and very briefly. Overall, 262 out of 276 toddlers successfully participated in the marked-mother task in at least one out of the two assessments (urban German = 99%, urban Indian = 97%, rural Indian = 87%, rural Nso = 95%).

Marked-Hand Assessments

In all of the rural Indian cohorts ($N = 54$) and in the 20- and 21-month-old rural Nso cohorts ($N = 40$), we administered the marked-hand task in the third and fourth assessments to determine whether toddlers were motivated to tactually explore a mark on their own bodies that they could see directly. After the MSR task was administered, the mirror was covered and the research assistant put some lipstick on her finger unbeknownst to the child. The research assistant then put a mark on the back of the toddlers' left hand when the toddler was distracted, or took both of the toddlers' hands with the toddlers' palms facing upwards and applied the mark to the back of the left hand. After marking the child's hand, the assistant played some games with the child focusing on hands and fingers (e.g., sticking flowers between fingers) for 5 min (or shorter if children showed clear signs of mark-directed behavior). It turned out to be somewhat problematic to get the toddlers to look at the mark on the back of their hand. Overall, 80 toddlers participated successfully in the marked-hand task at least once (rural Indian = 78%, rural Nso = 95%).

CODING

Toddlers' performance on each of the MSR, marked-mother, and marked-hand tasks, as well as the observation of other mirror behaviors was coded from videotape.

METHOD

MSR Assessments

Performance on the MSR tasks was coded by three German, three Indian, and one Nso research assistant. The coders coded the frequency of three types of mark-directed behavior: (a) localization—touching the mark directly or proximally (within 2 cm off the mark), (b) false localization—touching own face with an extended index finger further off the mark (>2 cm), and (c) showing—turning to another person and pointing toward own face. For about 20% of the total sample, touching own face with an extended index finger and turning to another person and pointing toward own face were also coded during phase 1 of the MSR task, that is, before the toddlers had a mark on their face. In the end, this subsample of toddlers did not exhibit any of the three mark-directed behaviors during phase 1 of the task. Therefore, we only coded children's behaviors during the second phase of the MSR task (i.e., when the child was marked) for all further analyses.

The children were assigned to one of two self-recognition statuses based on their mark-directed behavior: Children were classified as self-recognizers if they displayed at least one of the three mark-directed behaviors. Children who did not exhibit any of the mark-directed behaviors were classified as nonrecognizers. The coders also recorded the time when toddlers first looked at their own marked faces and the time when they first exhibited mark-directed behavior. Based on these two times we calculated latencies: the amount of time that elapsed between when the toddlers first looked at their marked face and their first mark-directed behavior.

In order to calculate inter-rater reliabilities, six coders (three German, three Indian) coded various subsets of the same data with regard to self-recognition status (recognizers vs. nonrecognizers), absolute frequencies for showing and localizing (separately for touching the mark and touching the face further off the mark), and looking-at-mark to touching-mark latencies (within a time tolerance of 3 s between coders). All three German coders coded a subset of the same German ($n = 90$) and rural Nso ($n = 60$) MSR assessments. While coding the rural Nso assessments, all unintelligible verbal utterances were coded and then checked and translated by one of the authors who is an Nso. All three Indian coders coded a subset of the same Delhi ($n = 60$) and rural Indian ($n = 60$) MSR assessments. The three German coders coded a further subset of the same urban ($n = 15$) and rural ($n = 15$) Indian MSR assessments that the Indian coders had coded and the three Indian coders coded a further subset of the same German MSR assessments that the German coders had coded ($n = 30$). The inter-rater reliabilities between all sets of coders were high for self-recognition status (percentage agreements >93%, Cohen's κs > .85), absolute frequencies for showing and localizing (Kendall's τs were >.63 and >.65, respectively), and

33

looking-at-mark to touching-mark latencies (i.e., proportions of agreement within a time tolerance of 3 s between coders were >92%).

Other Mirror Behavior

In addition to the analysis of the global indicators of self-recognition (i.e., mark-directed behavior), we examined other aspects of toddlers' behavior in front of the mirror, namely the toddlers' looking, experimenting, playmate, and pointing behavior. As a first step, we performed a microanalysis of the week 1 MSR assessments of same-aged toddlers (18- or 19-month olds) in two considerably different sociocultural contexts: the urban German context ($n = 40$) and the rural Nso context ($n = 40$). Based on these results, we developed a more coarse-grained coding scheme for the analysis of the six MSR assessments of all other age-cohorts from all sociocultural samples.

Two German research assistants coded five aspects of mirror behavior (in addition to mark-directed behavior) of the 18- and 19-month-old urban German and rural Nso toddlers. First, gaze was coded by timing the on- and offsets of all of the toddlers' looks at the mirror and, more specifically, at their specular image. Second, experimenting was coded by timing the on- and offsets of episodes in which toddlers experimented with their mirror image by moving their face, their head, or their body slower, faster, or more abruptly while keenly observing their specular image. Third, playmate behavior was coded by timing the on- and offsets of episodes in which toddlers treated the specular image as a peer, for example, by greeting the specular image or by offering an object (e.g., toy) to the specular image. Fourth, every occurrence of a pointing gesture (i.e., extended index finger) was coded as either self-referential pointing (toddlers pointing at themselves) or other-referential pointing (toddlers pointing at someone or something else). Finally, coders noted each occurrence of the following types of mirror-interaction behavior: (a) getting into the mirror—toddlers trying to get into the mirror by lifting their foot and trying to get "inside," (b) looking behind the mirror—toddlers first looking at their specular image and then walking around and looking behind the mirror, and (c) touching the mirror with the face—toddlers exploring the mirror orally by kissing or licking or by pressing their cheeks on the surface of the mirror.

In order to calculate inter-rater reliabilities, both coders coded 15 (seven urban German, eight rural Nso) of the 80 assessments for gaze. The inter-rater reliabilities between the two coders were high ($\kappa s > .88$). Given that behavior in the other four categories occurred relatively rarely, both coders coded 38 videos (22 urban German, 16 rural Nso). Inter-rater reliabilities were medium to high for experimenting ($\kappa s = .69$), playmate behavior ($\kappa s = .70$), pointing (Kendall's $\tau > .79$), getting into the mirror (Kendall's $\tau = .60$), looking behind the mirror (Kendall's $\tau = .81$), and touching the mirror with the face (Kendall's $\tau = .67$).

Based on the results of this two-sample microanalysis, we developed a coding scheme for all other cohorts and samples. The same coders who coded the absolute frequencies of mark-directed behavior (localizing and showing the mark) noted whether a number of behaviors occurred at least once. These behaviors included experimenting, playmate behavior, self-referential pointing, other-referential pointing, getting into the mirror, and looking behind the mirror. Inter-rater reliabilities were calculated based on the same MSR assessments that were coded by more than one coder to establish inter-rater reliabilities for mark-directed behavior. All reliabilities were greater than Cohen's $\kappa = .64$.

Marked-Mother Assessments

Performance on the marked-mother tasks was coded by two German, two Indian, and one Nso research assistant. The coders noted whether or not toddlers showed mark-directed behavior by pointing, touching, or manipulating the mark on their mother's face. In this way, the measure of mark-directed behavior on the marked-mother task was dichotomous: Toddlers who exhibited mark-directed behavior in at least one of the two marked-mother assessments versus toddlers who did not show mark-directed behavior in either assessment. As in the MSR task, the coders recorded the time when toddlers first looked at their mother's face and the time when they first exhibited mark-directed behavior. Based on the two times we calculated latencies: The amount of time that elapsed between when the toddlers first looked at their mother's marked face and their first mark-directed behavior.

In order to calculate inter-rater reliabilities, four coders (two German, two Indian) coded various subsets of the same data with regard to the presence of mark-directed behavior and looking-at-mark to touching-mark latencies (within a time tolerance of 3 s between coders). As was the case with the MSR assessments, both German coders coded a subset of the same German ($n = 25$) and rural Nso ($n = 25$) marked-mother assessments. While coding the rural Nso assessments, all unintelligible verbal utterances were coded and then checked and translated by one of the authors who is an Nso. Both Indian coders coded the same Delhi ($n = 20$) and rural Indian ($n = 20$) marked-mother assessments. The two German coders coded a further subset of the same urban ($n = 7$) and rural ($n = 8$) Indian marked-mother assessments that the Indian coders had coded. Likewise, the two Indian coders coded a further subset of the same German marked-mother assessments that the German coders had coded ($n = 15$). The inter-rater reliabilities between all sets of coders were high for the presence of mark-directed behavior (percentage agreements >98%, Cohen's κs > .84) and looking-at-mark to touching-mark latencies (proportions of agreement within a time tolerance of 3 s between coders were >91%).

Marked-Hand Assessments

Performance on the marked-hand tasks was coded by two German research assistants, two Indian research assistants, and one Nso research assistant. The coders noted whether or not toddlers showed mark-directed behavior by showing or touching the mark on their own hands. In this way, the measure of mark-directed behavior on the marked-hand task was dichotomous: Toddlers who exhibited mark-directed behavior in at least one of the two marked-hand assessments versus toddlers who did not show mark-directed behavior in either assessment. As in the MSR and marked-mother tasks, the coders recorded the time when toddlers first looked at the back of their left hand and the time when they first exhibited mark-directed behavior and calculated latencies between these two times.

Inter-rater reliabilities were calculated in the same way as in the marked-mother task. Inter-rater reliabilities between all sets of coders were high for the presence of mark-directed behavior (percentage agreements >95%, Cohen's κs > .81) and looking-at-mark to touching-mark latencies (proportions of agreement within a time tolerance of 3 s between coders were >88%).

RESULTS

In the following sections, we will present the analyses for the trajectories of mirror self-recognition both within (hypothesis 1) and between (hypothesis 2) sociocultural contexts. Furthermore, we will report the correlations between mirror self-recognition and pronoun use (hypothesis 3) and test the effects of mirror familiarity on mirror self-recognition as a potential alternative explanation of cross-cultural differences (hypothesis 4a). Next, we will report the results regarding toddlers' expressive behavior vis-à-vis their specular image and evaluate culture-specific norms of expressive behavior as an alternative explanation for cross-cultural differences in MSR (hypothesis 4b). Following these analyses, we will present the results of the marked-mother and the marked-hand tasks as indicators of toddlers' motivation for tactile exploration as the third alternative explanation of cross-cultural differences in MSR (hypothesis 4c). In a final set of logistic regression analyses, we will include all of the relevant predictors in order to explain interindividual and cross-cultural differences in MSR.

THE DEVELOPMENT OF MSR

Developmental Trajectories

There were two dichotomous MSR scores that we used to plot the trajectories of toddlers' self-recognition: (a) The percentage of toddlers in each cohort who recognized themselves at each assessment (MSR), and (b) cumulative self-recognizers (cMSR)—the percentage of toddlers in each cohort who recognized themselves in either a particular or at least one of the preceding assessments. In 2% ($n = 33$) of the assessments, the child did not look clearly enough at the mirror image of his or her face and, therefore, these assessments were excluded from further analyses. Children were assigned cumulative self-recognition status in omitted or excluded assessments if they had recognized themselves in an earlier assessment ($n = 39$).

Figure 1 shows the trajectories of MSR (left panel) and cMSR (right panel) for each cohort in the different Sociocultural Contexts (see Tables 4a and 4b

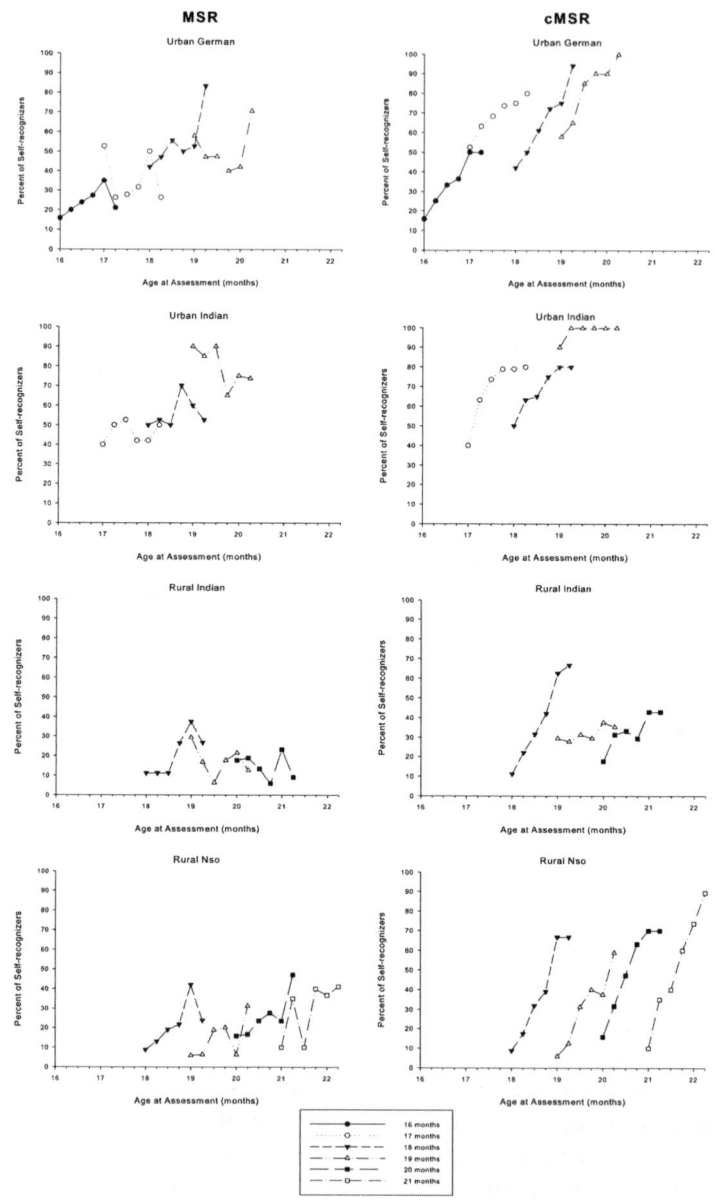

FIGURE 1.—Developmental trajectories for MSR (left) and cumulative MSR (right) as a function of age separately for age cohorts and each sociocultural context.

Note. For MSR, ns for each culture × cohort group ranged between 13 and 22. Only 9% of ns were smaller than $n < 18$. For cMSR, ns for each culture × cohort group ranged between 14 and 22. Only 7% of ns were smaller than $n < 18$. Decreases in cMSR are due to missing data of cumulative nonrecognizers in specific assessments.

TABLE 4a

PERCENTAGES OF TODDLERS EXHIBITING SELF-RECOGNITION (MSR) AND NUMBER OF MSR
ASSESSMENTS AT EACH OF THE SIX ASSESSMENTS SEPARATELY FOR AGE-COHORT AND
SOCIOCULTURAL CONTEXT

			MSR Assessment					
			1st	2nd	3rd	4th	5th	6th
Urban German								
16 months		MSR	15.8	20.0	23.8	27.3	35.0	21.1
		n	19 (21)	20 (21)	21	22	20 (21)	19 (22)
17 months		MSR	52.6	26.3	27.8	31.6	50.0	26.3
		n	19 (20)	19	18 (19)	19 (20)	20	19 (20)
18 months		MSR	42.1	47.1	55.6	50.0	52.6	83.3
		n	19	17 (19)	18 (19)	18 (19)	19	12 (13)
19 months		MSR	57.9	47.1	47.4	40.0	42.1	70.6
		n	19	17	19	20	19	17 (19)
Urban Indian								
17 months		MSR	40.0	50.0	52.6	42.1	42.1	50.0
		n	20	18 (19)	19 (20)	19 (20)	19 (20)	20
18 months		MSR	50.0	52.6	50.0	70.0	60.0	52.6
		n	20	19	20	20	20	19
19 months		MSR	90.0	85.0	90.0	65.0	75.0	73.7
		n	20	20	20	20	20	19
Rural Indian								
18 months		MSR	11.1	11.1	11.1	26.3	37.5	26.7
		n	18 (19)	18 (19)	18	19	16	15
19 months		MSR	29.4	16.7	6.3	17.6	21.4	12.5
		n	17 (18)	18	16 (17)	17	14 (17)	16 (17)
20 months		MSR	17.6	18.8	13.3	5.9	23.1	9.1
		n	17	16	15 (17)	17	13	11
Rural Nso								
18 months		MSR	8.7	13.0	19.0	21.7	42.1	23.8
		n	23	23	21	23	19	21
19 months		MSR	5.9	6.3	18.8	20.0	6.3	31.3
		n	17	16 (17)	16 (17)	15 (16)	16	16
20 months		MSR	15.8	16.7	23.5	27.8	23.5	47.1
		n	19	18	17	18	17	17
21 months		MSR	10.0	35.0	10.0	40.0	36.8	41.2
		n	20	20	20	20	19	17 (18)

Note. In some cases MSR was assessed but could not be considered in the analysis because toddlers did not look at their mirror image. In these cases the number of MSR assessments conducted is given in brackets.

for exact percentages and *n*s). Each data point represents the percentage of toddlers who recognized themselves in the mirror (each line therefore represents six MSR assessments).

Inspection of Figure 1 reveals five preliminary findings. First, there were higher proportions of self-recognizers and cumulative self-recognizers in the

39

TABLE 4b

PERCENTAGES OF TODDLERS EXHIBITING CUMULATIVE SELF-RECOGNITION (cMSR) AND NUMBER OF MSR ASSESSMENTS AT EACH OF THE SIX ASSESSMENTS SEPARATELY FOR AGE-COHORT AND SOCIOCULTURAL CONTEXT

		MSR Assessment					
		1st	2nd	3rd	4th	5th	6th
Urban German							
16 months	cMSR	15.8	25.0	33.3	36.4	50.0	50.0
	n	19 (21)	20	21	22	20 (21)	20 (22)
17 months	cMSR	52.6	63.2	68.4	73.7	75.0	80.0
	n	19 (20)	19	19	19 (20)	20	20
18 months	cMSR	42.1	50.0	61.1	72.2	75.0	94.1
	n	19	18 (20)	18 (19)	18 (19)	20	17 (18)
19 months	cMSR	57.9	65.0	85.0	90.0	90.0	100.0
	n	19	20	20	20	20	20
Urban Indian							
17 months	cMSR	40.0	63.2	73.7	78.9	78.9	80.0
	n	20	19 (20)	19 (20)	19 (20)	19 (20)	20
18 months	cMSR	50.0	63.2	65.0	75.0	80.0	80.0
	n	20	19	20	20	20	20
19 months	cMSR	90.0	100.0	100.0	100.0	100.0	100.0
	n	20	20	20	20	20	20
Rural Indian							
18 months	cMSR	11.1	22.2	31.6	42.1	62.5	66.7
	n	18 (19)	18 (19)	19	19	16	15
19 months	cMSR	29.4	27.8	31.3	29.4	37.5	35.3
	n	17 (18)	18	16 (17)	17	16 (18)	17 (18)
20 months	cMSR	17.6	31.3	33.3	29.4	42.9	42.9
	n	17	16	15 (17)	17	14	14
Rural Nso							
18 months	cMSR	8.7	17.4	31.8	39.1	66.7	66.7
	n	23	23	22	23	21	21
19 months	cMSR	5.9	12.5	31.3	40.0	37.5	58.8
	n	17	16 (17)	16 (17)	15 (16)	16	17
20 months	cMSR	15.8	31.6	47.4	63.2	70.0	70.0
	n	19	19	19	19	20	20
21 months	cMSR	10.0	35.0	40.0	60.0	73.7	89.5
	n	20	20	20	20	19	19 (20)

Note. In some cases MSR was assessed but could not be considered in the analysis because toddlers did not look at their mirror image often enough and had not recognized themselves in an earlier MSR assessment. In these cases the number of MSR assessments conducted is given in brackets.

older cohorts than there were in the younger cohorts. In addition, the proportion of self-recognizers within each age cohort increased with time. On a purely descriptive level, this age trend seemed more pronounced in the urban samples than it did in the rural samples. In particular, in the rural Indian sample, MSR rates did not seem to change much with age. Second, the proportions of self-recognizers (both MSR and cMSR) were higher in the urban German and urban Indian samples than they were in the rural Indian or rural Nso samples. Third, on visual inspection of the trendlines, there does not seem to be a larger increase in MSR over the 6 weeks for the rural samples (who had no prior mirror experience) compared to the urban samples. In addition, the percentage of self-recognizers of the same age (within each sociocultural sample) who had varying degrees of task familiarity (e.g., one or two assessments vs. five or six assessments)—the overlapping lines in Figure 1—did not seem to differ. Fourth, in the rural Nso sample, there was a sharp decrease in cMSR between same-aged toddlers in adjacent cohorts that was more pronounced than for all other samples. Finally, cMSR rates in the two urban samples show clear ceiling effects in the last assessments of the 19-month-old cohorts. This is not the case for the two rural samples, however. Specifically, self-recognition rates are still less than 50% in the rural Indian sample when toddlers are 21.5 months old for both MSR and cMSR. In the rural Nso sample, cMSR scores are around 90% in the last assessment of the 21-month-old cohort, that is, when toddlers are 22.25 months old. Despite this trend, not all toddlers had recognized themselves in the mirror at least once by then.

Mark-Directed Behavior

There were three types of mark-directed behavior that toddlers could exhibit: (a) Localization—touching the mark directly or proximally (≤ 2 cm), (b) false localization—touching own face with an extended index finger further off the mark (>2 cm), and (c) showing—turning to another person and pointing toward own face. In order to be classified as self-recognizers, children had to display at least one of the three mark-directed behaviors. Overall, there were 1,576 MSR assessments and toddlers qualified as self-recognizers (by exhibiting at least one of the mark-directed behaviors) in 35.52% of all MSR assessments ($n = 547$).

In order to determine whether there were sociocultural differences in the types of mark-directed behavior that self-recognizers exhibited, we subjected the number of passed MSR assessments (i.e., mark-directed behavior occurred at least once) to separate χ^2 tests. As shown in Table 5, in about 65% of passed MSR assessments, toddlers localized the mark at least once, irrespective of Sociocultural Context, $\chi^2 = 4.07$, *n.s.* The percentage of self-recognizers who exhibited false localization behavior did, however, differ as a function of Sociocultural Context, $\chi^2 = 8.55$, $p < .05$; as indicated by the superscripts in Table 5, the rural Indian toddlers exhibited false localization behavior less frequently than did toddlers from the two urban Sociocultural Contexts. Similarly, the percentage of self-recognizers who exhibited

TABLE 5

Average Percentages of Passed MSR Assessments in Which Toddlers Exhibited Localization, False Localization, and Showing Behavior at Least Once and Average Number of Occurrences of Each Behavior per MSR Assessment if Shown at Least Once as a Function of Sociocultural Context

	Urban German	Urban Indian	Rural Indian	Rural Nso
Percentage of self-recognizing toddlers exhibiting mark-directed behavior at least once				
Localization	61.3	61.2	68.6	71.3
False localization	58.0[a]	60.3[a]	39.2[b]	51.5[a,b]
Showing	42.5[a]	39.3[a]	19.6[b]	10.9[b]
Average number of occurrences (if shown at least once) per MSR assessment				
Localization	1.89 (1.22)[a]	2.52 (2.24)[b]	1.77 (1.33)[a,b]	2.08 (1.70)[a,b]
False localization	1.88 (1.54)	2.19 (2.08)	1.55 (.94)	1.81 (.86)
Showing	1.87 (1.20)	2.17 (1.69)	1.30 (.67)	1.09 (.30)

Note. Standard deviations are in parentheses. Superscripts of different letters indicate significant differences ($p < .05$) between the respective sociocultural samples (based on χ^2 tests for percentages and simple main effects testing with Bonferroni adjustment for averages).

showing behavior differed as a function of Sociocultural Context, $\chi^2 = 37.58$, $p < .01$; toddlers from the rural samples exhibited showing behavior less frequently than did toddlers from the urban samples. Note, however, that self-recognizers rarely exhibited showing behavior without also localizing the mark (urban German = 3.3%, urban Indian = 5.1%, rural Indian = 7.8%). We also analyzed whether toddlers differed in how often they showed specific types of mark-directed behavior (if they did so at least once) as a function of Sociocultural Context. To do so, we subjected the absolute number of occurrences of each of the mark-directed behaviors (per assessment in which this specific behavior occurred at least once) to separate ANOVAs. As shown in Table 5, the number of times that toddlers exhibited localization behavior differed as a function of Sociocultural Context, $F(3, 345) = 3.25$, $p < .05$; urban German toddlers exhibited less localizing behavior than did urban Indian toddlers. The number of times that toddlers exhibited showing behavior also differed as a function of Sociocultural Context, $F(3, 178) = 2.84$, $p < .05$, although post-hoc tests revealed no significant differences between the sociocultural samples. The number of times that toddlers exhibited false localization behavior did not differ as a function of Sociocultural Context, $F(3, 302) = 1.44$, $p > .05$.

Although there are some sociocultural differences in the proportions and absolute occurrences of the different types of mark-directed behavior, the *pattern* of mark-directed behavior was fairly similar across Sociocultural Contexts; in each Sociocultural Context, toddlers mostly exhibited localizing behavior followed by false localizing behavior and rarely exhibited showing behavior in the absence of any other kind of mark-directed behavior.

Latencies

We measured the time that elapsed from toddlers' first look at the mark to their first mark-directed behavior. In order to determine whether there were any sociocultural differences in the average looking-at-mark to touching-mark latencies, we subjected the latency data to a one-way (Sociocultural Context) ANOVA. The latency scores were log-transformed before they were entered into the analysis due to substantial positive skewness. The results of this analysis indicate that there were significant sociocultural differences in looking-at-mark to touching-mark latencies, $F(3, 388) = 2.83$, $p < .05$. On average, it took the rural Nso toddlers longer to touch the mark ($M = 42.37$ s, $SD = 61.49$ s) than it did any other sample (urban German: $M = 25.99$ s, $SD = 57.89$ s; urban Indian: $M = 23.12$ s, $SD = 58.28$ s; rural Indian: $M = 32.78$ s, $SD = 40.36$ gs), although none of the pairwise comparisons (with Bonferroni adjustment) reached conventional levels of statistical significance.

In order to determine whether toddlers localized the mark faster over the six consecutive MSR assessments, we subjected the log-transformed mean latency scores of the first 3 weeks versus the last 3 weeks to a 4 (Sociocultural Context) × 2 (Time: first 3 assessments vs. last 3 assessments) ANOVA with repeated measures over Time. We aggregated the latency data across the first three and the last three MSR assessments because there were very few self-recognizers in some of the samples. The results of this analysis indicate that there were no changes in toddlers' latency scores between the first three weeks of assessments and the last three weeks of assessments, $F(1, 72) = .99$, *n.s.*, and that this pattern was the same for each Sociocultural Context, $F(3, 72) = 2.11$, *n.s.*

EFFECTS OF AGE, GENDER, AND ASSESSMENT WEEK ON MSR

In order to determine whether the children's age, gender, and week of assessment (1–6) affected self-recognition rates, we subjected the MSR and cMSR scores to logistic regression analyses separately for each Sociocultural Context. With regard to MSR, there was a significant effect of age on MSR rates for the urban German, urban Indian, and rural Nso samples, but not for the rural Indian sample (see Table 6); older toddlers were more likely to be self-recognizers in each sample. We reanalyzed the rural Nso data excluding the 21-month-old data to make the two rural samples comparable with respect

TABLE 6

Odds Ratios (EXP(B)) of Age, Gender, and Week of Assessment for MSR and cMSR and Goodness of Fit Indicators for Logistic Regression Models

Sample	n	Odds Ratios—EXP(B)			Goodness of Fit	
		Age	Gender	Week	$\chi^2(4)$	R_N^2
MSR						
Urban German	449	1.52***	1.55*	.96	28.92***	.08
Urban Indian	352	2.17***	2.18**	.80**	40.21***	.15
Rural Indian	291	.86	2.25*	1.11	8.03*	.05
Rural Nso	448	1.22+	1.53+	1.27**	23.95***	.08
cMSR						
Urban German	476	1.98***	1.26	1.24**	88.09***	.23
Urban Indian	359	3.20***	5.07***	1.09	78.15***	.31
Rural Indian	306	.90	2.60***	1.37***	28.32***	.13
Rural Nso	468	1.33**	1.49+	1.67***	104.47***	.27

Note. Regression coefficients are indicated as odds ratios, that is, the amount the odds of being a self-recognizer are multiplied with when the predictor is incremented by a value of one unit. Age is in months and week of assessment is from 1 to 6. R_N^2 = Nagelkerke's R^2.
+$p < .10$; *$p < .05$; **$p < .01$; ***$p < .001$.

to participant age range. The significant age effect on MSR rates for the rural Nso sample disappeared after the 21-month olds were excluded, $EXP(B)$ = 1.12, *n.s.*, but the regression model was still significant, $\chi^2(4) = 16.51$, $p <$ .01. There were also significant effects of gender on MSR rates; girls from all of the sociocultural samples were more likely to be self-recognizers than were boys, smallest $EXP(B) = 1.53$, $p < .10$ (urban German: girls = 45.5%, boys = 35.0%; urban Indian: girls = 68.9%, boys = 52.6%; rural Indian: girls = 23.6%, boys = 11.9%; rural Nso: girls = 25.7%, boys = 18.8%; smallest $\chi^2 = 3.02$, $p_\text{1-sided} = .05$). There were significant effects of week of assessment for two of the sociocultural samples; there were fewer self-recognizers as the assessments progressed in the urban Indian sample, and there were more self-recognizers as the assessments progressed in the rural Nso sample (see Table 6). Note, however, that these effects were independent of any effects of age. For the different logistic regression models, Nagelkerke's R_N^2s—sometimes referred to as pseudo-R^2—ranged from $R_N^2 = .05$ (rural India) to $R_N^2 = .15$ (urban India).

The pattern of results was very similar for cMSR (see Table 6). Like the MSR results, there was a significant effect of age on cMSR scores for the urban German, urban Indian, and rural Nso samples, but not for the rural Indian sample; older toddlers were more likely to be cumulative self-recognizers in each sample. There were also significant effects of gender on cMSR rates; by the last MSR assessment, girls from the urban Indian, rural Indian, and rural Nso sociocultural samples were more likely to be cumulative self-recognizers than were boys (urban Indian: girls = 89.4%, boys = 68.2%; rural Indian: girls = 44.4%, boys = 24.5%; rural Nso: girls = 46.3%, boys = 38.3%), smallest $\chi^2 = 3.00$, $p_{\text{1-sided}} = .05$, whereas there were no significant differences between girls and boys in the urban German sample (girls = 64.9%, boys = 60.1%), $\chi^2 = 1.13$, $p > .05$. There were significant effects of week of assessment on rates of cMSR for the urban German, rural Indian, and rural Nso samples, smallest $EXP(B) = 1.24$, $p < .01$; there were more cumulative self-recognizers as the assessments progressed. There was no effect of week of assessment on cMSR rates for the urban Indian sample (see Table 6). For the different logistic regression models, Nagelkerke's R_N^2s ranged from $R_N^2 = .13$ (rural India) to $R_N^2 = .31$ (urban India).

Stability of MSR

We analyzed the stability of MSR across assessment weeks 2–6 by examining the consistencies of toddlers' self-recognition status between each specific week (MSR_t) and the previous week (MSR_{t-1}). Toddlers were classified as showing consistent behavioral responses in a specific week (MSR_t) if they either showed the same recognition status as in the week before: (a) nonrecognizers in both the specific week (MSR_t) and in the previous week (MSR_{t-1}), (b) self-recognizers in both the specific week (MSR_t) and in the previous week (MSR_{t-1}), or if successful mirror self-recognition emerged in-between successive weeks, (c) self-recognizers in the specific week (MSR_t) but not in the previous week (MSR_{t-1}). Toddlers were classified as showing inconsistent behavioral responses if they were self-recognizers in the previous week (MSR_{t-1}) but nonrecognizers in the specific week (MSR_t). Overall, in 88.2% of all assessments, toddlers showed a consistent pattern, regardless of sociocultural orientation (min = 86.7% in urban India, max = 90.9% in rural India). To evaluate the stability of MSR, we entered toddlers' self-recognition status (self-recognizer vs. nonrecognizer) in the preceding week (MSR_{t-1}) as a further predictor in the logistic regression analysis presented in Table 7. As shown in Table 7, MSR_{t-1} was the best predictor of MSR in all Sociocultural Contexts, smallest $EXP(B) = 1.89$, $p < .05$. The addition of the MSR_{t-1} term to the model also increased the proportion of variance explained to over .20 in all but the rural Nso sample. The relatively small odds ratio for MSR_{t-1} in the rural Nso sample indicates that MSR was least stable in this sample. This finding also explains the relatively large divergence between MSR and cMSR scores in the rural Nso sample (see Figure 1); although the MSR rates were below 50% for all weeks and cohorts, between 60% and 90% of the toddlers in each age cohort had recognized themselves at least once by the end of the study (cMSR).

TABLE 7

ODDS RATIOS ($EXP(B)$) OF MSR_{t-1} AGE, GENDER, AND WEEK OF ASSESSMENT FOR MSR AND GOODNESS OF FIT INDICATORS FOR LOGISTIC REGRESSION MODELS

Sample	n	Odds Ratios—$EXP(B)$				Goodness of Fit	
		MSR_{t-1}	Age	Gender	Week	$\chi^2(4)$	R_N^2
Urban German	373	5.73***	1.41**	1.46	1.05	81.03***	.26
Urban Indian	292	5.28***	1.54*	1.39	.85	63.02***	.26
Rural Indian	239	6.75***	.79	1.98+	1.20	32.58***	.21
Rural Nso	369	1.89*	1.20+	1.63+	1.19+	19.92***	.08

Note. Regression coefficients are indicated as odds ratios, that is, the amount the odds of being a self-recognizer are multiplied with when the predictor is incremented by a value of one unit. Age is in months and week of assessment is from 1 to 6. R_N^2 = Nagelkerke's R^2.
+$p < .10$; *$p < .05$; **$p < .01$; ***$p < .001$.

CROSS-CULTURAL DIFFERENCES IN THE DEVELOPMENT OF MSR

Preliminary Analysis of Caretakers' Socialization Goals

In the present study, we assessed the relative importance that mothers placed on autonomous and relational socialization goals (SGs) using a pairwise comparison procedure. We subjected the average scores for each of the eight SG items (four items on each of the autonomous and relational SG scales) and the mean score of the four autonomous SG items to separate one-way (Sociocultural Context) ANOVAs. As shown in Table 8, there were significant effects of Sociocultural Context on each of the SG items, smallest $F(3, 250) = 4.30$, $p < .01$, η_p^2s = .05–.54, and on the average rank for autonomous SG items, $F(3, 250) = 139.81$, $p < .001$, η_p^2s = .63. In general, the urban German mothers rated autonomous SGs as more important and relational SGs as less important than did mothers from either the rural Indian or the rural Nso samples. The scores of the urban Indian mothers fell intermediate to the scores of the urban German and rural samples. Specifically, urban Indian mothers valued some items to the same degree as did urban German mothers (autonomous SGs: development of personal interests, assertiveness; relational SGs: maintaining social harmony) and valued other items to the same degree as did rural Indian and rural Nso mothers (autonomous SGs: expression of own preferences). Several other items were valued by urban Indian mothers to intermediate degrees (autonomous SGs: being different from others; relational SGs: obedience, respect for elders).

Further inspection of Table 8 reveals that urban German mothers valued autonomous SGs over relational SGs. For example, the two most important SGs for urban German mothers were autonomous: That toddlers develop personal talents and interests and that they express their own

TABLE 8
Mothers' Average Scores for Autonomous and Relational Socialization Goals as a Function of Sociocultural Context

Socialization Goal	Urban German (n = 82)	Urban Indian (n = 47)	Rural Indian (n = 45)	Rural Nso (n = 80)
Autonomous Socialization Goals				
Develop personal interests	2.35 (2.16)[a]	1.40 (2.38)[a]	.07 (2.20)[b]	−.24 (2.42)[b]
Express own preferences	2.01 (2.37)[a]	−.19 (2.59)[b]	−.13 (1.85)[b]	−1.39 (3.14)[b]
Being different from others	−.94 (2.95)[a]	−2.74 (3.44)[b]	−5.22 (2.44)[c]	−4.80 (2.07)[c]
Assertiveness	−.10 (2.53)[a]	−1.19 (2.79)[a]	−4.07 (1.88)[b]	−4.68 (2.05)[b]
Relational Socialization Goals				
Sharing	1.05 (2.10)[a]	1.49 (2.73)[a,b]	1.51 (2.23)[a,b]	2.26 (1.78)[b]
Maintaining social harmony	.57 (2.68)[a]	−.21 (2.69)[a]	2.29 (1.94)[b]	2.78 (1.14)[b]
Obedience	−3.17 (2.77)[a]	.06 (3.29)[b]	2.82 (2.06)[c]	2.91 (1.77)[c]
Respect for elders	−1.78 (2.85)[a]	1.38 (2.35)[b]	2.73 (1.89)[c]	3.15 (1.21)[c]
Average Rank of Autonomous Socialization Goals				
Autonomous SGs	.83 (1.17)[a]	−.68 (1.50)[b]	−2.34 (1.19)[c]	−2.78 (1.04)[c]

Note. Standard deviations are in parentheses. Superscripts of different letters indicate significant differences ($p < .05$) between the respective sociocultural samples (based on simple main effects testing for averages with Bonferroni adjustment).

preferences. In contrast, mothers from both rural samples valued relational SGs over autonomous SGs. For example, the two most important SGs for rural Indian and rural Nso mothers were relational: That toddlers are obedient and that they have respect for elders. Urban Indian mothers valued aspects of both autonomous and relational SGs. For example, it was most important to urban Indian mothers that their children share with others (relational) and that they develop personal talents and interests (autonomous).

Taken together, these results support the hypothesis that the urban German sample has a prototypical autonomous orientation, the rural Nso and rural Indian samples have prototypical relational orientations, and the urban Indian sample has a hybrid autonomous-relational orientation.

Logistic Regression Analyses

We hypothesized that if the sociocultural environment affects the age at which MSR develops, then toddlers from urban Sociocultural Contexts (e.g., urban German, urban Indian) that emphasize autonomous SGs should recognize themselves earlier than should toddlers from rural Sociocultural Contexts (e.g., rural Indian, rural Nso) that emphasize relational SGs. Furthermore, the developmental course of self-recognition should not differ between the two autonomous Sociocultural Contexts (urban German and urban Indian) or between the two relational Sociocultural Contexts (rural India and rural Nso).

To test this hypothesis, we subjected the MSR and cMSR scores to logistic regression analyses. To do so, we compared only those age cohorts that were assessed in all four Sociocultural Contexts (i.e., 18- and 19-month-old toddlers). To account for culture in these analyses, we chose a contrast coding approach with three contrast variables (Cohen, Cohen, West, & Aiken, 2003). The central contrast code (C_{u-r}) contrasted the urban (urban German and urban Indian) versus rural (rural Indian and rural Nso) samples. The other two contrast variables compared the two urban samples (C_{wu}—within urban: urban German vs. urban Indian) and the two rural samples (C_{wr}—within rural: rural Indian vs. rural Nso). If, as we predicted, toddlers from urban Sociocultural Contexts recognize themselves earlier than do toddlers from rural Sociocultural Contexts, then the results of the logistic regression analyses should yield a significant effect for C_{u-r}. There should be no significant effects for the C_{wu} and C_{wr} contrast codes, however, if self-recognition does not differ between the two autonomous contexts and between the two relational contexts. Using hierarchical logistic regression analyses on self-recognition (MSR and cMSR), we entered age, gender, and week of assessment in step 1, C_{u-r} in step 2, C_{wu} and C_{wr} in step 3, the interaction coefficients of C_{u-r} and assessment week in step 4, and the interaction coefficient of C_{u-r} and age in step 5. The purpose of testing the interaction effects (C_{u-r} and age, C_{u-r} and assessment week) was to determine whether there were systematic differences between the urban and rural samples regarding changes in MSR with week of assessment or age.

The results of the hierarchical logistic regression analyses indicate that, after accounting for toddlers' age and gender and week of assessment in step 1, self-recognition rates (MSR and cMSR) were higher in the urban samples than they were in the rural samples (see significant odds ratios for C_{u-r} [step 2] in Tables 9 and 10). In step 3, the odds ratios for C_{wu} (within-urban contrast) were significant but the odds ratios for C_{wr} (within-rural contrast) were not. In other words, self-recognition rates (MSR and cMSR) did not differ between the two rural samples (consistent with our hypothesis). In contrast to our predictions, self-recognition rates (MSR and cMSR) did differ between the two urban samples; self-recognition rates were higher in the urban Indian sample than they were in the urban German sample.

With regard to the $C_{u-r} \times$ assessment week interaction, the increase in MSR over subsequent assessment weeks was significantly larger for the rural samples than it was for the urban samples. The $\Delta\chi^2$ score, however, indicated that the $C_{u-r} \times$ assessment week interaction resulted only in a marginally

RESULTS

TABLE 9
SUMMARY OF HIERARCHICAL LOGISTIC REGRESSION ANALYSIS FOR DEMOGRAPHIC AND CROSS-CULTURAL VARIABLES PREDICTING 18- AND 19-MONTH-OLD TODDLERS' MSR PERFORMANCE

Variable	Final $EXP(B)$	χ^2 (df)	$\Delta\chi^2$ (df)	R_N^2
Step 1				
Age	1.08	13.61 (3)**	—	.02
Gender	1.72**			
Week	1.63			
Step 2				
C_{u-r} (urban vs. rural)	7.30***	184.23 (4)***	170.62 (1)***	.26
Step 3				
C_{wu} (within urban)	.49***	196.81 (6)***	12.58 (2)**	.27
C_{wr} (within rural)	1.09			
Step 4				
C_{u-r} × week	.15**	200.06 (7)***	3.25 (1)+	.28
Step 5				
C_{u-r} × age	2.33***	206.88 (8)***	6.82 (1)**	.28

Note. $n = 879$. Regression coefficients are indicated as odds ratios ($EXP(B)$). Goodness of fit indicators were χ^2(df) = model-χ^2 ($D_{null} - D_k$) and $\Delta\chi^2$(df) = $\chi^2(m) = D_k - D_{(m+k)}$. R_N^2 = Nagelkerke's R^2. Assessment week was rescaled: 0 = week 1 to 1 = week 6. Age is in months. Interaction terms are based on centered scores.
+$p < .10$; **$p < .01$; ***$p < .001$.

TABLE 10
SUMMARY OF HIERARCHICAL LOGISTIC REGRESSION ANALYSIS FOR DEMOGRAPHIC AND CROSS-CULTURAL VARIABLES PREDICTING 18- AND 19-MONTH-OLD TODDLERS' cMSR PERFORMANCE

Variable	Final $EXP(B)$	χ^2 (df)	$\Delta\chi^2$ (df)	R_N^2
Step 1				
Age	1.92***	89.40 (3)***	—	.13
Gender	2.01***			
Week	4.38***			
Step 2				
C_{u-r} (urban vs. rural)	10.83***	291.89 (4)***	202.50 (1)***	.37
Step 3				
C_{wu} (within urban)	.47**	299.77 (6)***	7.87 (2)*	.38
C_{wr} (within rural)	1.08			
Step 4				
C_{u-r} × week	.08***	299.81 (7)***	.05 (1)	.38
Step 5				
C_{u-r} × age	8.00***	337.23 (8)***	37.42 (1)***	.42

Note. $n = 917$. Regression coefficients are indicated as odds ratios ($EXP(B)$). Goodness of fit indicators were χ^2(df) = model-χ^2 ($D_{null} - D_k$) and $\Delta\chi^2$(df) = $\chi^2(m) = D_k - D_{(m+k)}$. R_N^2 = Nagelkerke's R^2. Assessment week was rescaled: 0 = week 1 to 1 = week 6. Age is in months. Interaction terms are based on centered scores.
*$p < .05$; **$p < .01$; ***$p < .001$.

significant increase in the variance accounted for by step 4 of the logistic regression model (see Table 9). There was no interaction between assessment week and C_{u-r} for cMSR (see Table 10). In contrast, there were significant $C_{u-r} \times$ age interactions for both MSR and cMSR; the increases in MSR and cMSR with age were more pronounced in the urban samples than in the rural samples (see Tables 9 and 10). Note that the increase in the proportion of variance explained (R_N^2) for both MSR and cMSR was large when C_{u-r} was entered into the model in step 2 ($\Delta R_N^2 s = .24$), but did not increase much more when subsequent terms were entered into the model in steps 3–5 (largest $\Delta R_N^2 = .04$).

CROSS-CULTURAL VALIDITY OF MSR

As mentioned previously, research has shown that pronoun use is indicative of the emergence of an autonomous self-concept and that MSR correlates with pronoun use (Courage et al., 2004; LeVine, 1983; Lewis & Ramsay, 2004). Therefore, if MSR is a valid cross-cultural tool to measure toddlers' emerging self-awareness, MSR performance should be correlated with pronoun usage. To analyze the relation between pronoun use and self-recognition, we calculated partial correlations—controlling for the toddlers' age—between toddlers' pronoun usage scores and self-recognition (cMSR). Preliminary analyses indicated—in support of the validity of caretakers' reports of toddlers' pronoun usage—that there was a positive correlation between toddlers' age and pronoun use, $r = .24$, $p < .001$ (urban German: $r = .45$, $p < .001$, urban Indian: $r = .09$, n.s, rural Indian: $r = .10$, n.s, and rural Nso: $r = .24$, $p < .05$). In the urban German sample, there were significant correlations between pronoun usage and cMSR for assessments 1–4 (see Table 11). There were mainly positive though nonsignificant correlations between pronoun usage and cMSR for the urban Indian sample. In the rural Indian sample, there were significant correlations between pronoun usage and cMSR for all six assessments. In the rural Nso sample, there were significant correlations between pronoun usage and cMSR for assessments 4–6. Thus, there were consistent positive correlations, especially in the rural samples, between pronoun use and self-recognition. Where there were nonsignificant correlations between pronoun use and cMSR, this was, in part, related to absolute frequencies of self-recognition status in specific weeks within samples. For example, in the earlier assessments, there were hardly any self-recognizers in the rural Nso sample, whereas in the later assessments there were hardly any nonrecognizers in the urban German sample. On a more descriptive level, Table 11 shows the percentages of self-recognizers versus nonrecognizers who used pronouns (according to their caretakers' reports). In all but one case,

TABLE 11
Partial Correlations Controlling for Age Between Pronoun Use and Self-Recognition (cMSR) and Percentages of Self-Recognizers Versus Nonrecognizers Who Use Pronouns at Each of the Six Assessments as a Function of Sociocultural Context

Week of Assessment	Urban German	Urban Indian	Rural Indian	Rural Nso
1st	.24††	.13	.20†	.07
	(78.1% vs. 46.5%)†††	(60.0% vs. 44.4%)	(90.0% vs. 68.6%)	(71.4% vs. 57.6%)
2nd	.16†	.06	.30††	.08
	(71.8% vs. 47.2%)††	(54.8% vs. 45.5%)	(92.9% vs. 62.5%)††	(70.6% vs. 56.4%)
3rd	.20††	−.03	.33††	.04
	(70.8% vs. 37.9%)†††	(45.5% vs. 55.6%)	(93.3% vs. 62.1%)††	(63.0% vs. 56.8%)
4th	.15†	−.01	.38†††	.17†
	(69.8% vs. 37.5%)†††	(52.8% vs. 50.0%)	(94.1% vs. 60.0%)††	(69.4% vs. 48.6%)†
5th	.13	.06	.38†††	.22††
	(67.2% vs. 40.0%)††	(54.1% vs. 40.0%)	(90.0% vs. 57.1%)††	(69.8% vs. 46.2%)††
6th	.12	.08	.33††	.23††
	(67.7% vs. 28.6%)†††	(55.3% vs. 40.0%)	(90.0% vs. 63.6%)††	(68.0% vs. 40.0%)††

Note. †$p < .10$, one-tailed. ††$p < .05$, one-tailed. †††$p < .01$, one-tailed.

the percentage of toddlers' who used pronouns was higher for self-recognizers than for nonrecognizers. Furthermore, in 14 out of 24 cases this difference was significant.

THE EFFECT OF MIRROR FAMILIARITY ON TODDLERS' RECOGNITION STATUS

We predicted that if mirror familiarity affects toddlers' capacity for MSR, there should be a significant interaction between culture (urban vs. rural) and week of assessment. Specifically, the self-recognition rates of toddlers from rural contexts (e.g., rural Nso and rural Indian), who have no previous mirror experience but who develop increasing familiarity with mirrors, should increase at a faster rate than should the recognition rates of toddlers from urban contexts (i.e., urban German and urban Indian). In this way, any differences in self-recognition rates across successive weeks in the urban samples can be solely attributed to normal developmental processes. In contrast, differences in self-recognition rates across successive weeks in the rural samples can be attributed to normal developmental processes *plus* increasing mirror familiarity. As mentioned above, the results of the hierarchical regression analysis indicate that there were no $C_{u-r} \times$ assessment week interactions for either MSR or cMSR (see Tables 8 and 9). Thus, any change in MSR rates over the assessment period (for both the urban and rural samples) were probably due to normal developmental processes rather than increasing mirror familiarity.

Another way in which we determined whether mirror familiarity influenced self-recognition was to compare the self-recognition rates (MSR) of same-aged toddlers who had different degrees of mirror and task familiarity within each sociocultural sample (see overlapping lines in Figure 1). Due to the cross-sequential design of the present study and its overlapping age-cohorts, the fifth and sixth MSR assessments of one cohort could be compared with the first and second MSR assessments of the next older cohort, as these toddlers were the same age. The urban toddlers were sufficiently familiar with mirrors given that they are exposed to mirrors from an early age. Children from the rural samples had no, or very little, mirror experience prior to participating in the present study, however. In this way, differences in MSR rates between the first and second MSR assessments and the fifth and sixth assessments in the urban samples could be interpreted as effects of task familiarity rather than as effects of mirror familiarity. Differences in MSR rates between the first and second MSR assessments and the fifth and sixth MSR assessments in the rural samples, however, could be interpreted as effects of task familiarity plus increasing mirror familiarity.

There were 20 comparisons in self-recognition rates of same-aged toddlers in different stages of MSR assessments (first and second assessments vs. fifth and sixth assessments). There were significant differences in MSR rates for four comparisons. First, in the urban German sample, 19.25-month-old toddlers (who started at 18 months) at their sixth MSR assessment recognized themselves more often (83.8%) than did 19.25-month-old toddlers (who started at 19 months) at their second MSR assessment (47.1%), $\chi^2 = 3.93$, $p < .05$. Second, in the rural Nso sample, 19-month-old toddlers (who started at 18 months) at their fifth MSR assessment recognized themselves more often (42.1%) than did 19-month-old toddlers at their first MSR assessment (5.9%), $\chi^2 = 3.93$, $p < .05$. Finally, there were two significant effects on MSR rates for the urban Indian sample; 19- and 19.25-month-old toddlers at their first (90%) or second (85%) MSR assessments recognized themselves more often than did 19- and 19.25-month-old toddlers (who started at 18 months) at their fifth (60%) or sixth (52.6%) MSR assessments, smallest $\chi^2 = 4.80$, $p < .05$. Note, however, that as soon as we adjusted for α-error inflation, none of these differences reached significance.

To summarize, neither the nonsignificant effect of the interaction term ($C_{u-r} \times$ week) in the logistic regression analyses nor the direct comparison of recognition rates of same-aged toddlers with different degrees of mirror and task familiarity support mirror familiarity as a potential explanation of cross-cultural differences in recognition rates.

RESULTS

TODDLERS' EXPRESSIVE BEHAVIOR VIS-À-VIS THEIR SPECULAR IMAGE—RELATION TO RECOGNITION-STATUS AND SOCIOCULTURAL CONTEXT

Contrasting Urban German and Rural Nso Toddlers

In addition to mark-directed behavior, we observed other aspects of toddlers' behavior in front of the mirror, namely their looking, experimenting, playmate, and pointing behavior. To do so, we microanalyzed the week 1 MSR assessments of same-aged toddlers (18- or 19-month-olds) in two considerably different Sociocultural Contexts: the urban German context ($n = 40$) and the rural Nso context ($n = 40$).

Self- and Mark-Directed Behavior

During the first assessment of the 18- and 19-month-old toddlers, 50% ($n = 20$) of the urban German children recognized themselves but only 7.5% ($n = 3$) of the rural Nso children recognized themselves, $\chi^2 = 17.42$, $p < .001$ (see Table 12). All self-recognizers (in both samples) localized the mark on their face by touching their face with an extended index finger between 1 and 8 times in the urban German sample and either once or twice in the rural Nso sample. In addition, 23% of the urban German toddlers (45% of the self-recognizers) showed the mark to their mothers once or twice by turning to and looking at their mothers while pointing to their own face. None of the three rural Nso self-recognizers exhibited this behavior. As discussed in the Method section, these behaviors (touching face with an extended index finger or turning to mother while pointing to one's face) never occurred during the first phase of the MSR task (without mark). None of the rural Nso toddlers but six (15%) of the urban German toddlers said their name in front of the mirror. Of these six toddlers, five also showed mark-directed behavior and were thus classified as self-recognizers.

Gaze Behavior

Rural Nso toddlers looked at the mirror and at their mirror image about three times longer than did urban German toddlers (see Table 12). The proportion of time that toddlers looked at their own mirror image was subjected to a 2 (Phase: With mark vs. without mark) × 2 (Sociocultural Context: Urban German vs. rural Nso) ANOVA with repeated measures over Phase. The results of this analysis indicate that there were significant main effects of Sociocultural Context, $F(1, 77) = 31.64$, $p < .001$, $\eta_p^2 = .29$, and Phase, $F(1, 77) = 7.30$, $p < .01$, $\eta_p^2 = .09$, on the proportion of time that toddlers looked at their mirror image. These effects were qualified by a Phase × Sociocultural

TABLE 12

MICROANALYSIS OF ASSESSMENT 1 DATA FROM 18- AND 19-MONTH OLDS IN THE URBAN GERMAN AND RURAL NSO SAMPLES

Mirror Behavior	Urban German	Rural Nso	$t(77)$ or χ^2
Average phase duration of MSR task (min)			
Phase 1—without mark	18.31 (4.68)	18.61 (4.98)	−.27
Phase 2—with mark	5.38 (5.07)	5.37 (1.72)	.01
Gaze behavior (% of time)			
Looking at mirror	16.7 (7.6)	41.9 (14.1)	−9.93***
Looking at specular image	8.3 (4.4)	23.5 (11.2)	−8.04***
Mark-directed behavior (% ≥ 1)			
Localizing mark	39.5	7.5	11.22**
False localization	21.1	2.5	6.57*
Total localization	50	7.5	17.42***
Showing mark	22.5	0	10.14**
Saying own name	15	0	6.49*
Mirror interaction (% ≥ 1)			
Experimenting	17.5	75.0	26.60***
Playmate	17.5	82.5	33.80***
Other mirror behavior (% ≥ 1)			
Look behind mirror	40.0	50.0	.81
Get into mirror	7.5	22.5	3.53+
Touch mirror with face	37.5	42.5	.21
Pointing behavior (% ≥ 1)			
Self-referential pointing	65.0	47.5	2.49†
Other-referential pointing	37.5	37.5	.00

Note. Standard deviations are in parentheses. % ≥ 1 = percentage of toddlers that showed the target behavior at least once. Significant differences are based on χ^2 tests for mark-directed behavior, mirror interaction behavior, pointing behavior, and other mirror behavior, and simple *t*-tests for phase duration and gaze behavior.
†$p < .10$, one-tailed. +$p < .10$, two-tailed. *$p < .05$, two-tailed. **$p < .01$, two-tailed. ***$p < .001$, two-tailed.

Context interaction, $F(1, 77) = 9.18$, $p < .01$, $\eta_p^2 = .11$; the rural Nso toddlers looked at their mirror image for about the same proportion of time in the two phases (without mark: $M = 23.4\%$, $SD = 12.8\%$; with mark: $M = 22.9\%$, $SD = 12.9\%$) but the urban German toddlers looked at their mirror image for a greater proportion of time when they had a mark on their face ($M = 15.4\%$, $SD = 13.5\%$) than when they had no mark on their face ($M = 7.1\%$, $SD = 3.8\%$). The increase in looking at one's mirror image between the no-mark and mark phases within the urban German sample was due to the finding that self-recognizers spent significantly more time looking at their mirror image once they had a mark on their face (without mark: $M = 7.6\%$, $SD = 3.9\%$; with mark: $M = 19.1\%$, $SD = 14.4\%$), $t(19) = 3.99$, $p < .01$. In contrast, nonrecognizers spent the same amount of time looking at their mirror image regardless of phase (without mark: $M = 6.5\%$, $SD = 3.6\%$; with mark: $M = 11.8\%$, $SD = 11.6\%$), $t(18) = 1.98$, $p > .05$.

RESULTS

Experimenting Behavior

As shown in Table 12, the majority of rural Nso toddlers but only some of the urban German toddlers showed experimenting behavior at least once. Of the toddlers who exhibited experimenting behavior, the rural Nso toddlers engaged in experimenting behavior for longer ($M = 34.95$ s, $SD = 30.11$ s) than did the urban German toddlers ($M = 11.33$ s, $SD = 7.67$ s), $t(35) = 3.80$, $p < .01$.

Playmate Behavior

As shown in Table 12, a significantly higher proportion of rural Nso toddlers than urban German toddlers showed playmate behavior at least once. Of the toddlers who exhibited playmate behavior, the rural Nso toddlers engaged in playmate behavior for longer ($M = 57.28$ s, $SD = 63.64$ s) than did the urban German toddlers ($M = 5.84$ s, $SD = 7.06$ s), $t(38) = 4.51$, $p < .001$. There were also qualitative differences in playmate behavior between the urban German and the rural Nso samples. For example, some of the rural Nso toddlers explicitly addressed the "other" child in the mirror by offering objects to their mirror image while saying, "Kóh!," (Take!). Other utterances, which occurred less often, were, "Leey!" (Look!), "Weey!" (Put!), or "Á dú!" (Go away!). In the urban German sample, playmate behavior usually consisted of holding out an object playfully or "greeting" the other child by smiling.

Other Mirror Behavior

Other behavior patterns that support the observation that some toddlers treated their specular image like another child were getting into and looking behind the mirror. As shown in Table 12, there was a marginally significant tendency for more rural Nso toddlers than urban German toddlers to try to get into the mirror. A similar percentage of toddlers in both Sociocultural Contexts looked behind the mirror at least once, but of those who did so, rural Nso toddlers were more persistent and did so more often ($M = 5.80$, $SD = 5.59$) than did the urban German toddlers ($M = 1.88$, $SD = 1.50$), $t(34) = 3.01$, $p < .01$. Similarly, equal proportions of rural Nso toddlers and urban German toddlers touched the mirror with their faces (see Table 12). Once again, rural Nso toddlers showed this behavior more often ($M = 14.53$, $SD = 10.94$) than did urban German toddlers ($M = 3.27$, $SD = 3.49$), $t(30) = 4.02$, $p < .01$.

Pointing Behavior

As shown in Table 12, a higher percentage of urban German toddlers pointed at their mirror images (self-referential pointing) at least once than did rural Nso toddlers. Toddlers pointed to someone or something else (other-referential pointing) equally often in the two samples. Within the urban German sample, there were no differences between self-recognizers and non-recognizers in any of these behaviors (experimenting, playmate, pointing, or other mirror behavior) except toddlers' gaze.

Behavior Patterns Between Sociocultural Contexts and Across Time

Based on the results of the two-sample microanalysis presented above, we developed a coding scheme for all other cohorts and samples. In this analysis, coders noted whether a number of behaviors occurred at least once. These behaviors included experimenting, playmate behavior, self-referential pointing, other-referential pointing, getting into the mirror, and looking behind the mirror.

Incidence of Mirror Behaviors

The experimenting, playmate, pointing, and other mirror interaction behaviors occurred to varying degrees in the different cultural contexts (see Table 13). Overall, each of these behaviors was exhibited by only a minority of toddlers. As shown in Table 13, experimenting and playmate behavior occurred more often in the rural samples than it did in the urban samples (urban samples: $\max_{exp} = 35\%$ of the 17-month-old urban Indian children in week 1, $\max_{play} = 10\%$ of 16-month-old urban German children in week 2). The maximum values across Sociocultural Contexts and assessment weeks for other mirror behaviors were: 53% of toddlers showed at least one instance of self-referential pointing (19-month-old urban German children in week 5), 37% of toddlers pointed at least once to someone or something else (19-month-old urban German children in week 5), 24% of toddlers tried to get into the mirror at least once (20-month-old rural Indian children in week 1), and 25% of toddlers looked behind the mirror at least once (17-month-old urban Indian children in week 1). On average, the urban German and rural Nso toddlers exhibited more self- and other-referential pointing than did the urban or rural Indian toddlers. Furthermore, the urban German toddlers tried to get into the mirror less often than did toddlers from any other sociocultural sample. Finally, the urban German and rural Nso toddlers looked behind the mirror more often than did the urban or rural Indian toddlers.

RESULTS

TABLE 13

PERCENTAGES OF MSR ASSESSMENTS IN WHICH TARGET MIRROR BEHAVIORS OCCURRED AT LEAST ONCE AS A FUNCTION OF SOCIOCULTURAL CONTEXT

Mirror Behaviors	Urban German ($n = 467$)	Urban Indian ($n = 356$)	Rural Indian ($n = 302$)	Rural Nso ($n = 452$)	χ^2
Experimenting[1]	12.8^a	20.7^b	25.4^b	30.8^c	23.62***
Playmate[1]	3.4^a	1.1^a	14.8^b	57.0^c	353.99***
Self-ref. pointing	27.9^a	16.5^b	16.5^b	32.4^a	40.25***
Other-ref. pointing	10.2^a	6.3^b	6.8^b	16.1^c	26.03***
Get into mirror	1.3^a	5.1^b	5.5^b	6.7^b	16.29**
Look behind mirror	12.4^a	6.5^b	4.5^b	10.7^a	17.80***

[1] The mirror behavior data from the 18- and 19-month olds in the urban German and the rural Nso samples were only coded in the microanalysis (see Table 12). Therefore, ns are 246 and 222, respectively. Superscripts of different letters indicate significant differences between the respective sociocultural samples (based on χ^2 tests and logistic regression analyses).
** $p < .01$; *** $p < .001$.

To further analyze the incidence of these mirror behaviors, we computed separate hierarchical logistic regression analyses. The model comprised of culture (contrast categories C_{u-r}, C_{wu}, C_{wr}, as described above) (step 1), followed by the toddlers' age, self-recognition status (MSR), and week of assessment (step 2), and the interaction between C_{u-r} and week of assessment (step 3). As in the previous analyses, interaction terms were computed with centered scores.

Experimenting Behavior

In step 1, the C_{u-r} (urban vs. rural) and C_{wu} (within urban) contrast coefficients were significant predictors of experimenting behavior; odds ratios were $EXP(B) = .50$, $p < .001$, for C_{u-r} and $EXP(B) = .56$, $p < .05$, for C_{wu}, $\chi^2 = 24.55$, $p < .001$, $R_N^2 = .03$. The contrast codes and post-hoc χ^2 tests indicate that experimenting behavior occurred significantly less often in the urban German sample than it did in the urban or rural Indian samples. Experimenting behavior occurred most often in the rural Nso sample (see Table 13). In steps 2 and 3, neither the toddlers' age, self-recognition status, week of assessment, nor the $C_{u-r} \times$ week interaction were significant predictors of experimenting behavior.

Playmate Behavior

In step 1, the C_{u-r} (urban vs. rural) and C_{wr} (within rural) contrast coefficients were significant predictors of playmate behavior; odds ratios were

$EXP(B) = .04$, $p < .001$, for C_{u-r} and $EXP(B) = .13$, $p < .001$, for C_{wr}, $\chi^2 = 323.99$, $p < .001$, $R_N^2 = .43$. The contrast codes and post-hoc χ^2 tests indicate that all Sociocultural Contexts differed significantly from each other except for the two urban samples; playmate behavior occurred least often in the urban Indian and urban German samples, followed by the rural Indian sample and then the rural Nso sample (see Table 13). In step 2, age, but not self-recognition status or week of assessment, was a significant predictor of playmate behavior, $EXP(B) = .68$, $p < .05$. In general, more younger toddlers showed playmate behavior at least once than did older toddlers (e.g., urban German: 16-month-olds = 4%, 17-month-olds = 3%; urban Indian: 17-month-olds = 3%, 18- to 19-month-olds = 0%; rural Indian: 18-month-olds = 22%, 19-month-olds = 11%, 20-month-olds = 10%; rural Nso: 20- to 21-month-olds = 57%). The increase in Nagelkerke's R^2 between steps 1 and 2 was rather small, however, $\Delta\chi^2(3) = 8.97$, $p < .05$, $\Delta R_N^2 = .01$. In step 3, the C_{u-r} × week interaction was not a significant predictor of playmate behavior.

Self-Referential Pointing

In step 1, the C_{wr} (within rural) and C_{wu} (within urban) contrast coefficients were significant predictors of self-referential pointing; odds ratios were $EXP(B) = 1.93$, $p < .001$, for C_{wu} and $EXP(B) = .42$, $p < .001$, for C_{wr}, $\chi^2 = 40.71$, $p < .001$, $R_N^2 = .04$. The contrast codes and post-hoc χ^2 tests indicate that self-referential pointing occurred significantly more often in the urban German and the rural Nso samples than it did in the two Indian samples (see Table 13). In step 2, self-recognition status, $EXP(B) = 1.92$, $p < .001$, and week of assessment, $EXP(B) = .87$, $p < .01$, were significant predictors of self-referential pointing, $\Delta\chi^2(3) = 34.60$, $p < .001$, $\Delta R_N^2 = .03$. Overall, more self-recognizers than nonrecognizers exhibited self-referential pointing (urban German: self-recognizers = 35.4%, nonrecognizers = 22.4%; urban Indian: self-recognizers = 17.3%, nonrecognizers = 15.2%; rural Indian: self-recognizers = 23.5%, nonrecognizers = 15.0%; rural Nso: self-recognizers = 47.5%, nonrecognizers = 28.0%). Self-referential pointing also decreased from week 1 to week 6 (week 1 = 29%, week 2 = 26%, week 3 = 26%, week 4 = 23%, week 5 = 20%, week 6 = 19%). This pattern was the same in the urban versus rural samples (step 3).

Other-Referential Pointing

In steps 1 and 2, culture and assessment week significantly predicted other-referential pointing, step 1: $\chi^2 = 26.51$, $p < .001$, $R_N^2 = .04$; step 2:

$\Delta\chi^2(3) = 10.15$, $p < .05$, $R_N^2 = .05$. In step 1, the C_{wr} (within rural) and C_{wu} (within urban) contrast coefficients were significant predictors of other-referential pointing; odds ratios were $EXP(B) = 1.84$, $p < .05$, for C_{wu} and $EXP(B) = .40$, $p < .01$, for C_{wr}. The contrast codes and post-hoc χ^2 tests indicate that rural Nso toddlers exhibited other-referential pointing most often, followed by urban German toddlers and then urban Indian and rural Indian toddlers (see Table 13). In step 2, week of assessment was a significant predictor of other-referential pointing, $EXP(B) = .88$, $p < .05$; other-referential pointing decreased from week 1 to week 6 (week 1 = 13%, week 2 = 8%, week 3 = 13%, week 4 = 9%, week 5 = 11%, week 6 = 7%). This pattern was the same in the urban versus rural samples (step 3).

Trying to Get Into the Mirror

The urban German toddlers generally tried to get into the mirror less often than did toddlers from the other cultural contexts, $EXP(B) = .43$, $p < .01$, for C_{u-r} and $EXP(B) = .25$, $p < .01$, for C_{wu}, $\chi^2 = 19.28$, $p < .001$, $R_N^2 = .04$ (see Table 13).

Looking Behind the Mirror

The urban German and rural Nso toddlers looked behind the mirror more often than did toddlers from either of the Indian samples, $EXP(B) = 1.96$, $p < .05$, for C_{wu} and $EXP(B) = .39$, $p < .01$, for C_{wr}, $\chi^2 = 17.79$, $p < .001$, $R_N^2 = .03$ (see Table 13).

TODDLERS' MOTIVATION FOR TACTILE EXPLORATION

Marked-Hand Assessments

In all of the rural Indian cohorts and some of the rural Nso cohorts (20- and 21-month olds), we administered the marked-hand task in weeks 3 and 4. We did this to determine whether toddlers' motivation—or lack thereof—to tactually explore a mark on their body might be an alternative explanation for the low self-recognition rates observed in the two rural samples. Overall, 80 toddlers participated in the marked-hand task at least once (rural Indian: $n = 42$, 78%; rural Nso: $n = 38$, 95%). Of these toddlers, 74% (rural Indian = 76%, rural Nso = 71%) exhibited mark-directed behavior in at least one of the assessments. We subjected toddlers' performance in the marked-hand task to a logistic regression analysis with sociocultural context (rural India vs. rural Nso), age cohort, and gender as predictors. None of these factors were significant predictors of performance in the marked-hand task. There were no effects of age or gender on performance in the marked-hand task.

There were, however, significant differences in the time it took toddlers to show their first mark-directed behavior, $t(57) = -3.57$, $p < .001$. Due to substantial positive skewness, the latency scores were log-transformed before they were entered into the analysis. Untransformed mean scores indicate that it took Nso toddlers significantly longer ($M = 47.19$ s, $SD = 53.52$ s) than it took rural Indian toddlers ($M = 11.56$ s, $SD = 18.47$ s) to show a reaction toward the mark after looking at their marked hand for the first time.

Correlations (contingency coefficients) between performance on the marked-hand task and cMSR (week 1 to week 6) ranged from $r_{CC} = .00$ to $r_{CC} = .16$ (ps $=$ n.s.) for the rural Indian sample and from $r_{CC} = .22$ (n.s.) to $r_{CC} = .39$ ($p < .05$) for the rural Nso sample. Correlations (contingency coefficients) between performance on the marked-hand task and MSR (week 1 to week 6) ranged from $r_{CC} = .00$ to $r_{CC} = .18$ (ps $=$ n.s.) for the rural Indian sample and from $r_{CC} = .11$ (n.s.) to $r_{CC} = .35$ ($p < .05$) for the rural Nso sample. In this way, self-recognition rates were somewhat higher for the Nso subsample of toddlers who referred to the mark on the back of their hand than they were for those who did not show mark-directed behavior toward their hand. Thus, it seems as if touching the mark on the back of their hands was related to whether or not toddlers showed mark-directed behavior, but only in the rural Nso sample. This finding, while interesting, only explains cross-cultural differences in self-recognition to a certain degree for two reasons: (a) the recognition rates of rural Indian toddlers were unaffected by their performance on the marked-hand task, and (b) the recognition rates of rural Nso toddlers (20- and 21-month olds) who passed the marked-hand task still fell below those of toddlers in the urban samples (18- and 19-month olds).

Marked-Mother Assessments

In all of the samples, we administered the marked-mother task in weeks 2 and 6 to see whether toddlers would refer to a mark on their mother's face. Overall, 262 toddlers participated in the marked-mother task at least once (urban German: $n = 81$, urban Indian: $n = 58$, rural Indian: $n = 47$, rural Nso: $n = 76$). Of these toddlers, about 85% of the urban toddlers (urban German $= 83\%$, urban Indian $= 90\%$) and 50% of the rural toddlers (rural Indian $= 49\%$, rural Nso $= 51\%$) referred to the mark on their mothers' faces by either pointing to or touching the mark, $\chi^2 = 38.71$, $p < .001$. We subjected toddlers' performance in the marked-mother task to a logistic regression analysis with sociocultural context (C_{u-r}, C_{wu}, and C_{wr}), age cohort, and gender as predictors. Only the odds ratio of C_{u-r} (urban vs. rural) reached significance, $EXP(B) = 5.81$, $p < .001$, $\chi^2(5) = 42.30$, $p < .001$, $R_N^2 = .21$; urban toddlers were more likely to show mark-directed behavior in the marked-mother task than were rural toddlers. There was no effect of age or gender on performance in the marked-mother task.

There were significant differences in the time it took toddlers to show their first mark-directed behavior, $F(3, 169) = 7.69$, $p < .001$. Due to substantial positive skewness, the latency scores were log-transformed before they were entered into the analysis. Pairwise comparisons (with Bonferroni adjustment) indicate that rural Nso toddlers reacted significantly slower ($M = 52.66$ s, $SD = 62.21$ s) than did urban German toddlers ($M = 24.99$ s, $SD = 46.50$ s) or urban Indian toddlers ($M = 11.13$ s, $SD = 18.83$ s). On a descriptive level, rural Nso toddlers also reacted slower than did rural Indian toddlers ($M = 23.05$ s, $SD = 28.70$ s).

Correlations between performance on the marked-mother task and cMSR (week 1 to week 6) ranged from $r_{CC} = .02$ (rural Nso sample, week 5) to $r_{CC} = .24$ (rural Indian sample, week 1) ($ps = n.s.$). Similarly, correlations between performance on the marked-mother task and MSR (week 1 to week 6) were all insignificant with two exceptions: the urban German sample (week 6), $r_{CC} = .26$, $p < .05$, and the rural Nso sample (week 6), $r_{CC} = .32$, $p < .05$. Note, however, that as soon as we adjusted for α-error inflation, none of these correlations reached significance. Thus, although there were cross-cultural differences in the percentage and latencies of mark-directed behavior in the marked-mother task, these differences were not related to cross-cultural differences in toddlers' performance on the MSR task.

Taken together, the findings concerning the marked-hand and marked-mother tasks indicate that culture-specific norms of expressive behavior in the form of motivation for tactile exploration do have a significant, although moderate, effect on MSR rates.

EXPLAINING INTERINDIVIDUAL AND CROSS-CULTURAL DIFFERENCES IN MIRROR SELF-RECOGNITION

Based on theoretical considerations, we have argued that there are various potential theories that may explain the cross-cultural differences found in mirror self-recognition, namely: (a) culture-specific emphases on autonomous SGs and associated conceptions of the self, (b) familiarity with mirrors, (c) norms of expressive behavior, and (d) motivation for tactile exploration. In our final analysis, therefore, we analyzed the extent to which these factors accounted for the cross-cultural variation in mirror self-recognition. As shown in Tables 9 and 10, logistic regression analyses on MSR and cMSR indicated that sociocultural context (rural vs. urban sociocultural samples) was the best predictor of mirror self-recognition and greatly contributed to the proportion of variance explained ($\Delta R_N^2\text{s} = .24$). To analyze which factors underlie these cross-cultural differences, each of the aforementioned factors was included in the analysis if it met the minimum requirement that it correlated with mirror self-recognition within at least one of the Sociocultural Contexts. This minimum requirement was necessary in order to show that the variable under question is a potential mechanism that is causally related to toddlers' performance during the MSR assessments. If this requirement is not met the logistic regression analysis could yield significant regression coefficients, which may only be pseudorelations, based solely on cross-cultural mean differences in both the dependent and independent variables.

The analyses presented above suggest that neither norms of expressive behavior (e.g., playmate, experimenting, or pointing behavior) nor familiarity with mirrors influenced cross-cultural differences in MSR. With regard to motivation for tactile exploration, however, the two significant correlations of this variable with MSR suggest that there might be a moderate effect of such a motivation on MSR performance. Therefore, this variable has been included in the analyses.

According to our interpretation, mothers' emphasis on autonomous SGs is an index of how important it is for mothers that their children develop a sense of themselves and others as autonomous intentional agents. Therefore, these SGs should be directly related to toddlers' MSR performance both within and across cultures. To test for within-culture relations between maternal SGs and toddlers' performance in the MSR assessments, we included maternal SGs as a predictor in the logistic regression models presented in Table 6. Using hierarchical logistic regression analyses on self-recognition (MSR and cMSR), we entered age, gender, and week of assessment in step 1 and the mean score of the four autonomous SGs in step 2. With regard to MSR, there was a significant effect of autonomous SGs on MSR rates for both rural samples (see Table 14); as expected, an emphasis on autonomous SGs was positively associated with self-recognition. With regard to cMSR, there was a significant effect of autonomous SGs on MSR rates for the urban German and the rural Indian sample. While the effect was as expected for the rural Indian sample, there was a negative association between autonomous SGs and self-recognition in the urban German sample. Overall, there is positive evidence from two of the four samples that caretakers' emphasis on autonomous SGs is positively associated with self-recognition.

Extending the hierarchical logistic regression analyses presented in Tables 9 and 10, we entered toddlers' motivation for tactile exploration (as assessed by the marked-mother task) and caretakers' emphasis on autonomous SGs in step 2, after accounting for toddlers' age and gender and week of assessment in step 1. In the final step, we entered the three contrast codes

RESULTS

TABLE 14
Summary of Hierarchical Logistic Regression Analyses for Demographic Variables and Autonomous Socialization Goals Predicting Toddlers' MSR (Upper Half) and cMSR (Lower Half) Performance Separately for Sociocultural Contexts

MSR	Urban German ($n = 449$)	Urban Indian ($n = 276$)	Rural Indian ($n = 242$)	Rural Nso ($n = 448$)
Step 1 ($\chi^2(3)$ (R_N^2))	28.92*** (.08)	23.76*** (.11)	6.04 (.04)	23.95*** (.08)
Age	1.53***	2.09***	.88	1.05
Gender	1.56*	1.54+	2.24*	1.41
Week	.96	.85*	1.08	1.32***
Step 2 ($\Delta\chi^2(4)$ (R_N^2))	1.11 (.09)	1.39 (.12)	20.53*** (.17)	6.86** (.10)
Autonomous SGs	.91	.90	1.85***	1.41**
cMSR	Urban German ($n = 467$)	Urban Indian ($n = 277$)	Rural Indian ($n = 249$)	Rural Nso ($n = 464$)
Step 1 ($\chi^2(3)$ (R_N^2))	88.09*** (.23)	62.28*** (.31)	32.05*** (.17)	104.47*** (.27)
Age	2.04***	3.35***	.85	1.28*
Gender	1.24**	1.14	1.46***	1.70
Week	1.23	3.30**	3.41***	1.46
Step 2 ($\Delta\chi^2(4)$ (R_N^2))	12.76*** (.27)	.16 (.31)	21.99*** (.27)	1.51 (.27)
Autonomous SGs	.72***	1.04	1.75***	1.09

Note. Regression coefficients are indicated as odds ratios (*EXP(B)*), that is, the amount the odds of being a self-recognizer are multiplied with when the predictor is incremented by a value of one unit. Goodness of fit indicators were $\chi^2(\text{df}) = \text{model-}\chi^2 (D_{null} - D_k)$ and $\Delta\chi^2(\text{df}) = \chi^2(m) = D_k - D_{(m+k)}$. R_N^2 = Nagelkerke's R^2. Assessment week was rescaled: 0 = week 1 to 1 = week 6. Age is in months.
+$p < .10$; **$p < .01$; ***$p < .001$.

for culture (C_{u-r}, C_{wu}, and C_{wr}) to identify how much intercultural variance remains unaccounted for. Given that standardized regression coefficients are a matter of some complexity in logistic regression analysis, we followed the approach suggested by Cohen et al. (2003) and Pampel (2000) and z-standardized all predictors. The resulting regression coefficients describe the change in the logit for a one-standard-deviation change in the predictors. This method allows for an approximate comparison of the relative influences of the two predictors (marked mother and autonomous SGs) entered in step 2.

The results of the hierarchical logistic regression analyses indicate that, after accounting for toddlers' age and gender and week of assessment in step 1, self-recognition rates (MSR and cMSR) were significantly and positively associated with both step 2 predictors (marked-mother task and autonomous SGs) (see Table 15). The associated increase in the proportion of variance explained (R_N^2) was significant and large for both MSR and cMSR ($\Delta R_N^2\text{s} = .20$). In terms of predicting MSR, the odds ratios of performance in the marked-mother task and autonomous SGs were approximately equal, suggesting relatively equal strength of these predictors of MSR. The cMSR

TABLE 15

SUMMARY OF TWO HIERARCHICAL LOGISTIC REGRESSION ANALYSES FOR DEMOGRAPHIC AND CROSS-CULTURAL VARIABLES PREDICTING 18- AND 19-MONTH-OLD TODDLERS' MSR AND cMSR PERFORMANCE

	MSR		cMSR	
Variable	Final $EXP(B)$	$\Delta\chi^2$(df) (R_N^2)	Final $EXP(B)$	$\Delta\chi^2$(df) (R_N^2)
Step 1				
Age	1.04	7.61$^+$(.01)	1.25$^+$	77.99*** (.13)
Gender	1.10		1.14	
Week	1.22$^+$		2.00***	
Step 2				
Marked mother	1.40**	116.89***(.21)	1.22*	140.40*** (.33)
Autonomous SGs	1.51**		1.92***	
Step 3				
C_{u-r} (urban vs. rural)	1.80***	52.51*** (.28)	1.84***	51.98*** (.40)
C_{wu} (within urban)	.69***		.63***	
C_{wr} (within rural)	.95		.88	

Note. $n = 753$ for MSR and $n = 773$ for cMSR. Regression coefficients are indicated as odds ratios ($EXP(B)$). Goodness of fit indicators were χ^2 (df) = model-χ^2 ($D_{null} - D_k$) and $\Delta\chi^2$(df) = $\chi^2(m) = D_k - D_{(m+k)}$. R_N^2 = Nagelkerke's R^2. All predictors were z-standardized.
$^+p < .10$; $^*p < .05$; $^{**}p < .01$; $^{***}p < .001$.

analysis, in contrast, indicates that the predictive power of autonomous SGs was, on a descriptive level, higher compared to that of performance on the marked-mother task.

Another way of thinking about the relative contribution of the step 2 predictors (performance on marked-mother task and autonomous SGs) is to compare the degree to which each variable is predictive of MSR performance over and above the other (see Cohen et al., 2003). As shown in Table 15, the overall fit after entering the step 2 variables in the regression model increased by $\Delta\chi^2(2) = 116.89$ for MSR and by $\Delta\chi^2(2) = 140.40$ for cMSR. If one enters the step 2 predictors separately (i.e., as two separate steps in the hierarchical regression analysis) and further compares their relative contributions to the model depending on the order in which the two predictors are entered, the following picture emerges: If performance on the marked-mother task is entered first, the overall fit increases by $\Delta\chi^2(1) = 57.73$, $p < .001$, $\Delta R_N^2 = .10$ for MSR and by $\Delta\chi^2(1) = 46.84$, $p < .001$, $\Delta R_N^2 = .07$ for cMSR. If autonomous SGs are entered in the next step, the overall fit further increases by $\Delta\chi^2(1) = 59.16$, $p < .001$, $\Delta R_N^2 = .10$ for MSR and by $\Delta\chi^2(1) = 93.57$, $p < .001$, $\Delta R_N^2 = .13$ for cMSR. If, however, autonomous SGs are entered first, the overall fit increases by $\Delta\chi^2(1) = 88.90$, $p < .001$, $\Delta R_N^2 = .15$ for MSR and by $\Delta\chi^2(1) = 124.82$, $p < .001$, $\Delta R_N^2 = .18$ for cMSR. If performance on the marked-mother task is entered in the next step, the overall fit further increases by $\Delta\chi^2(1) = 27.99$, $p < .001$, $\Delta R_N^2 = .05$ for MSR and by $\Delta\chi^2(1) = 15.59$, $p < .001$, $\Delta R_N^2 = .02$ for cMSR. These results indicate that both autonomous SGs and performance on the marked-mother task contribute to the model over and above each other. Furthermore, the relative increase of predictiveness is considerably higher for autonomous SGs than it is for performance on the marked-mother task. Specifically, the increase in the degree of additional variance explained is relatively small if performance on the marked-mother task is entered into the regression analysis after accounting for autonomous SGs.

Returning to the hierarchical regression analyses presented in Table 15, a further important finding is that there is still cross-cultural variation that is not accounted for by performance on the marked-mother task and autonomous SGs. When we entered the categorical variables for culture in step 3, the overall fit of the model increases further for both MSR and cMSR. This increase is, however, smaller (largest $\Delta R_N^2 s = .07$) compared to the increase obtained in step 2. Similar to the analyses presented in Tables 9 and 10, self-recognition rates were higher in the urban samples than they were in the rural samples (see significant odds ratios for C_{u-r}). Furthermore, the odds ratios for C_{wu} (within-urban contrast) were significant but the odds ratios for C_{wr} (within-rural contrast) were not. In other words, after accounting for the effects of performance on the marked-mother task and autonomous SGs, self-recognition rates (MSR and cMSR) were higher in the urban Indian sample than they were in the urban German sample. Consistent with our hypothesis, self-recognition rates did not differ between the two rural samples.

DISCUSSION

The focus of the present study was to trace the development of mirror self-recognition during the second year of life in four different sociocultural contexts that emphasize the development of autonomy to very different degrees. In the sections that follow, we will discuss the main findings concerning cross-cultural similarities and differences in the age of emergence, the stability of mirror self-recognition, and toddlers' expressive behavior vis-à-vis their specular image. We will also discuss findings concerning the cross-cultural validity of mirror self-recognition as an indicator of toddlers' awareness of themselves (and others) as autonomous intentional agents.

CULTURE-SPECIFIC DEVELOPMENTAL PATHWAYS OF MSR

The results of the present study are in line with our cultural precocity assumption; an autonomous self-concept, as measured by MSR, develops earlier in those sociocultural contexts in which caretakers emphasize autonomous socialization goals. Specifically, growing up in an urban, middle-class family (urban German, urban Indian) compared to growing up in a rural, subsistence-based environment (rural Nso, rural Indian) accounted for a considerable proportion of the total variance in the cohorts of 18- and 19-month-old toddlers. The cross-cultural regression analyses on MSR and cMSR indicate that Nagelkerke's R_N^2s increased by .24 after entering intercultural contrasts into the model. These intercultural differences (i.e., autonomy-supporting vs. relational) explained far more variance than did the specific autonomy-supporting or relational cultural contexts toddlers came from. These intercultural differences also explained far more variance than did any other variable, namely, age, gender, or week of assessment.

The analysis of caretakers' socialization goals clearly confirmed the theoretically proposed cultural models for each of the sociocultural contexts. Urban German mothers prioritized autonomous socialization goals and differed significantly from mothers from both of the rural sociocultural contexts on each of the eight socialization goals. Caretakers from the rural

DISCUSSION

sociocultural contexts showed a clear preference for relational socialization goals; relative ranks were all negative or close to zero for autonomous socialization goals. As expected, urban Indian mothers expressed preferences that were intermediate to those of mothers from the urban German and rural samples. For some socialization goals, the relative ranks of the urban Indian mothers were similar to those of the urban German mothers (e.g., develop personal talents and interests). For most other socialization goals, relative ranks of the urban Indian mothers differed significantly from those of mothers from both the urban German and the two rural samples (e.g., do what parents say). One has to keep in mind, however, that because we used a pairwise comparison procedure, the scores are relative scores, that is, the importance of one specific socialization goals compared to all other socialization goals. Thus, these relative scores do not allow us to definitively conclude that for urban German caretakers, autonomous socialization goals were, in absolute terms, more important than they were for urban Indian caretakers. Rather, urban German mothers clearly prioritize autonomous socialization goals—just as caretakers from the rural samples clearly prioritize relational socialization goals—while urban Indian mothers show more balanced preferences.

Based on these results, we propose that particular aspects of the sociocultural context (i.e., the socialization goals that caretakers hold), have a profound influence on children's sociocognitive development, especially their emerging sense of themselves and others as autonomous intentional agents. This interpretation is further supported by the final regression analyses showing that autonomous socialization goals were the best predictor of mirror self-recognition and—together with toddlers' motivation for tactile exploration (see below)—explained most of the cross-cultural variation in MSR performance. Further support for the interpretation that MSR develops precociously in autonomous sociocultural contexts comes from the finding that levels of mirror self-recognition of the oldest cohorts in the relational sociocultural contexts (20- and 21-month-olds) were comparable to those of the youngest cohorts in the autonomy-supporting sociocultural contexts (16- and 17-month-olds). Taken together, these findings lend strong support to our argument that generalizations based exclusively on data from Western settings (i.e., autonomous orientations) do not adequately describe the development of MSR in relational sociocultural contexts. As the results of the present study demonstrate, self-recognition rates differ between samples as a function of the samples' sociocultural orientations. A revision of the dominant conclusion regarding the development of MSR in developmental psychology is clearly warranted; MSR develops between 15 and 24 months (on average at 18–19 months) *given a strong normative emphasis on the toddlers' autonomy*. If this normative emphasis is missing, or different, as it is in prototypical relational sociocultural contexts, only a minority of 19-month-olds will recognize themselves in a mirror (Keller et al., 2004; Keller, Kärtner et al., 2005) and their developmental trajectories may take a different course.

POTENTIAL MECHANISMS UNDERLYING THE EFFECT OF CULTURE

The results of the present study indicate that it is the relative importance attributed to the development of autonomy that best explains cross-cultural differences in MSR. The question remains, however, as to what the specific mechanisms are that underlie the effect of culture. What are the behavioral correlates of caretakers' differential emphases on autonomous socialization goals that drive their children's development in the first $2^1/_2$ years of life?

In an initial attempt to answer this question, Keller et al. (2004) found that mothers' autonomy-promoting behavior toward their 3-month-olds was related to the toddlers' MSR rates when they were 19 months old across three different cultural contexts. In another study, Keller, Kärtner et al. (2005) found that mothers' level of visual contingent responsiveness during interactions with their 3-month-olds was higher in an autonomous sociocultural context than it was in a relational sociocultural context and, furthermore, predicted toddlers' mirror self-recognition at 19 months. The authors suggested that this distal parenting style with its focus on visual contingent responsiveness, face-to-face interactions, and object stimulation supports infants' sense of self-efficacy and, hence, their development of autonomy as indexed by MSR.

On the basis of our findings, we argue that MSR does not reflect (secondary) representational capacity per se, but a specific representation, namely the representation of the self as an autonomous intentional agent that is based on emerging self-awareness. Thus, not only do toddlers need to possess the ability for secondary representation but they also need a specific object or state to represent, in this case their own mental states (intentional and affective). We believe that it is not necessarily toddlers' general representational capacity that differs across cultures but toddlers' awareness of themselves, especially self-awareness of their internal states.

This specific type of self-awareness is the result of social interaction, which enables toddlers to conceive of themselves as selves in the minds of others (Rochat & Zahavi, 2011). As the results of the present study suggest, this development is highly contingent on toddlers' sociocultural context. Keller and her colleagues have suggested that visual contingent responsiveness during face-to-face interactions may be a potential mechanism by which caretakers foster children's sense of themselves. What are the specific mechanisms within these episodes of intense face-to-face interaction that affect toddlers' sense of themselves? In autonomous sociocultural contexts, caretakers typically focus on children's internal mental states (intentional and affective); they verbalize and respond to the anticipated initiatives, intentions, wishes, and preferences of the infant (Keller, 2007). Thus, caretakers in autonomous sociocultural contexts typically direct infants' and toddlers' attention to their own internal states (Demuth, 2008). In this way, toddlers are sensitized to intentional and affective self-states, which they consequently become increasingly aware of (e.g., social biofeedback model; Gergely & Watson, 1996, 1999).

Furthermore, there is extensive literature on the key role that triadic interaction, pretense, and imitation play in toddlers' further sociocognitive development during the late first and early second years (Meltzoff, 2007a, 2007b; Tomasello, 2008; Tomasello, Carpenter, Call, Behne, & Moll, 2005). For example, in their model of sociocognitive development, Barresi and Moore (1996) suggest that triadic interaction and object-directed imitation are key mechanisms that foster the transition from shared intentional relations (early second year) to an understanding of self and other as autonomous intentional agents (middle of the second year). By sharing others' focus of attention and by imitating others' object-directed behavior, toddlers accumulate interpersonal experience and come to habitually complement the observed behavior by ascribing subjective experience to the other person.

Another possible mechanism that may explain cross-cultural differences in toddlers' development of a sense of themselves as autonomous intentional agents is the degree to which specific social practices such as triadic interaction or infants' goal- or object-directed imitation are appreciated and encouraged in specific sociocultural contexts. In most relational sociocultural contexts, pretense and symbolic play is barely tolerated, if not discouraged, and toddlers only rarely engage in such activities (Gaskins, 1999). Gaskins further notes that in many traditional cultures (e.g., the Kaluli, Somoans, Gusii, and Mayans), parents almost never play with objects with their young infants because adult play with children is inappropriate; children are expected to adapt to the adult world, not vice versa (Gaskins, Haight, & Lancy, 2006). Future research should aim to identify parenting strategies during the first $2^1/_2$ years of life that foster the development of autonomy in children and that may account for the cross-cultural differences in toddlers' self-awareness during the second year.

AGE OF EMERGENCE

In order to identify different focal windows for the emergence of MSR, we began by tracing the development of MSR in cohorts of 16- and 17-month-olds in the autonomy-supporting urban contexts and followed toddlers from the relational contexts up to the age of 22.25 months. We believed that this design would allow us to trace the full developmental trajectories of MSR for children from different sociocultural environments. In addition, we hypothesized that age-dependent increases in MSR rates in the relational sociocultural contexts would substantiate the validity of the mark-and-mirror test across different sociocultural contexts.

In support of these considerations, we found clear effects of toddler age on MSR rates for urban German, urban Indian, and rural Nso toddlers. We did not find any effect of toddler age on MSR rates for the rural Indian sample, however. In contrast to the rural Nso sample, there was no cohort of 21-month-olds in the rural Indian sample; it is possible that we did not follow the rural Indian toddlers for long enough to observe the critical, focal age range for the development of MSR in this sample. This interpretation was supported by additional regression analyses in which we excluded the 21-month-old rural Nso toddlers' data. After these toddlers were excluded, the age effect was no longer significant for the rural Nso sample. Thus, the increase in MSR with age in the rural Nso sample generally supported the validity of the mark-and-mirror test as an age-sensitive tool for this particular aspect of children's sociocognitive development (i.e., self- and other-awareness). Note, however, that the sensitive periods for the development of MSR differ substantially across samples with different sociocultural orientations.

STABILITY OF MSR AND DIVERGENCE OF MSR AND cMSR SCORES

Another important issue in the interpretation of the present results is the stability of MSR across time and the interpretation of MSR versus cMSR scores. The best predictor of MSR in a specific week was the MSR score in the previous week. As the divergence of MSR and cMSR scores indicates, however, there is no perfect stability in the sense of a Guttman scale across time. Rather, the regression analyses indicate that MSR was moderately stable across assessment weeks. Generally, there are two different ways of interpreting these moderate, but imperfect, stabilities. The first interpretation is methodological, the second more theoretical. There are different implications depending on the different interpretations of these findings.

First, one could argue from a methodological point of view that it is generally unlikely that the mark-and-mirror test is perfectly reliable. Situational factors such as the toddlers' mood or motivation or factors such as the toddlers' shyness, expressiveness, or activity might all affect toddlers' behavior during the mark-and-mirror test. There may be other factors that increase measurement error and that are related to the fact that the test was administered repeatedly at relatively short 7-day intervals. For example, toddlers' motivation might fade because they simply get bored of the task over time. Finally, there could be other situational demands that lead to culture-specific measurement errors, which could explain the relatively lower stability of MSR in the rural Nso sample.

DISCUSSION

If one favors this interpretation, the divergence between MSR and cMSR scores would be due to measurement error. As a consequence, cMSR, and not MSR, would be the relevant indicator of toddlers' emerging sense of self; a toddler should be categorized as a self-recognizer even if he or she does not show mark-directed behavior in a subsequent test. From this perspective, one of the main findings of the present study is that by the end of the six mark-and-mirror test assessments, all of the 19-month-olds and at least 80% of the 18-month-olds recognized themselves at least once in the urban German and urban Indian samples, whereas only 59–67% of the rural Nso and about 35–67% of the rural Indian toddlers did so. Thus, cMSR rates were higher in the two autonomy-supporting contexts than they were in the two relational sociocultural contexts. Furthermore, MSR rates in the two autonomy-supporting contexts were also higher than are MSR rates in most other studies that have examined the development of MSR so far (see Table 1). These studies have shown that MSR rates of 18- to 20-month-old toddlers were somewhere between 25% and 65%. Therefore, it is likely that, due to measurement error, earlier studies significantly underestimated the percentage of self-recognizers in their samples. Future studies should aim to assess MSR over a number of assessments in order to increase the reliability of the findings.

Second, one could argue from a theoretical perspective that every developmental achievement necessarily oscillates before it stabilizes. From this dynamic systems perspective, variability is a fundamental property of development; there is empirical evidence that stable advances in performance are preceded by periods of instability and variability (Courage et al., 2004; Thelen & Smith, 1994; van Geert, 1991; van Geert & van Dijk, 2002). The results of the present study show that there is culture-specific variation in the degree to which toddlers' performance on the MSR task varies over time. As the regression analyses on the stability of MSR indicated, MSR was least stable in the rural Nso sample. On visual inspection of Figure 1, one can easily see this effect in the relatively larger differences in cMSR rates between age cohorts, that is, larger vertical distances between overlapping lines. This interpretation of intraindividual variability as a fundamental property of development is further supported by Courage et al.'s (2004) findings; they assessed toddlers' MSR bi-weekly from 15 to 23 months of age and found that toddlers started as stable nonrecognizers, underwent a phase of instable MSR, and finally emerged as stable self-recognizers.

From a dynamic systems perspective, one could further argue that there is less intraindividual stability, that is, more oscillation, between developmental statuses (self-recognizer vs. nonrecognizer) in those contexts in which there is less external or environmental support that would help to stabilize toddlers' emerging developmental attainment of MSR. If one interprets MSR as a behavioral index of self-awareness and an understanding of the self as an autonomous agent, then one could argue that the reason for the unstable MSR rates in the rural Nso sample is that there is much less socialization pressure on the toddler; Nso caretakers generally offer less experiences that are critical for toddlers to develop such an understanding. In the autonomy-supporting contexts, on the other hand, caretakers invest much more effort into socializing their children toward autonomy, which is conducive to the emergence and maintenance/stabilization of these developmental attainments. For example, mothers in these sociocultural contexts refer to their children's mental states often, they require toddlers to make choices and personal decisions from early on, and they treat their children as quasi-equal interaction partners (Keller, 2007). If the toddlers' social environment does not provide such experiences (or only infrequently), the development of a sense of self as an autonomous agent develops incidentally and the transitory phase shows a more erratic pattern.

One has to keep in mind, however, that the rural Indian toddlers' performance during the mark-and-mirror test was similar to the performance of toddlers' performance in the two autonomy-supporting cultural contexts (in terms of stability). Does this finding pose a problem for the interpretation that there is less stability and more intrapersonal variation in developmental domains that are not supported by the specific socialization agenda of a given sociocultural context? In our view, this finding would pose a problem, but only if the performance *level* (i.e., MSR rates) was also similar to that of the autonomy-supporting contexts. In the present study, it seems that the majority of toddlers from the autonomy-supporting sociocultural contexts recognized themselves in the mirror and their recognition rates were relatively stable, whereas the majority of toddlers from the rural Indian sample were stable nonrecognizers. Within the different age cohorts in the rural Indian setting, there was more variation and higher cMSR performance in the youngest cohort (18-month-olds). The pattern for this cohort is comparable to the 18-month-olds in the rural Nso setting in terms of MSR rates and divergence of MSR versus cMSR scores. The 19- and 20-month-old rural Indian toddlers, however, seem to be predominantly stable nonrecognizers.

At this point, we can only offer a cautious interpretation of both the different stabilities of the rural Nso versus the rural Indian samples and the different stabilities of the youngest versus the older age cohorts within the rural Indian sample. Taking into account Courage et al.'s (2004) findings that toddlers start as nonstable recognizers and then proceed gradually to stable self-recognition, one could argue that there is a certain threshold that needs to be met in order to set off certain developmental processes. Accordingly, it is possible that the majority of the rural Indian toddlers had not yet met this threshold by the end of the 6 weeks. The MSR rates of the rural Nso toddlers were above 20% for most weeks, whereas the MSR rates of the rural Indian toddlers were below 20% for most weeks, with the exception of the youngest age cohort. Note that it was this youngest cohort whose developmental course of cMSR was atypical compared to the other rural Indian age cohorts. It was, however, similar to the developmental course of cMSR within the rural Nso age cohorts. In this sense, one could speculate that the rate of self-recognizers as a cohort-based criterion indexes a threshold that needs to be met before the onset of dynamic developmental processes. These processes, in turn, may contribute to toddlers' development of self-awareness and a sense of themselves as autonomous agents.

TODDLERS' EXPRESSIVE BEHAVIOR VIS-À-VIS THEIR SPECULAR IMAGE

In addition to cross-cultural differences in MSR, there were cross-cultural differences in the frequency and duration of other behavioral patterns that toddlers showed in front of the mirror. Specifically, playmate and experimenting behavior were most often exhibited by rural Nso toddlers followed by rural Indian toddlers. Thus, in the two rural samples, more toddlers showed behaviors that tested the perfect contingency of their specular image and treated their specular image as a social partner. This cross-cultural difference in expressive behavior, which can be broadly characterized as one of urban versus rural sociocultural contexts, most likely stems from differential degrees of mirror familiarity between the contexts. In the rural settings, toddlers were generally more interested in the mirror and in their specular image. For example, in the microanalysis comparing rural Nso with urban German toddlers, rural Nso toddlers looked at the mirror and at their specular image about three times longer than did the urban German toddlers. This heightened interest seems to lead to both more experimenting and more playmate behavior, which goes against the common assumption that experimenting (contingency testing) and playmate behavior are antagonistic behavioral patterns (Amsterdam, 1972; Bischof-Köhler, 1989; Dixon, 1957; Lewis & Brooks-Gunn, 1979; see also Povinelli, Rulf, Landau, & Bierschwale, 1993). According to this assumption, experimenting should be associated with self-recognition but nonrecognizers should be more likely to treat their specular image as another child. We did not find any support for this assertion, however. Instead, our findings show that there were no systematic differences within cultural contexts in either playmate or experimenting behavior patterns as a function of toddlers' self-recognition status (recognizer vs. nonrecognizer). The only behavioral pattern that was associated with MSR status was self-referential pointing. The common assumption in the literature is that if toddlers do not understand that it is themselves in the mirror, they are more likely to point at their mirror image when observing the mark (e.g., Bischof-Köhler, 1989). To the best of our knowledge, there is no empirical evidence for this assertion. In fact, our findings suggest the opposite; being a self-recognizer was positively associated with self-referential pointing. Thus, it may actually be the case that when toddlers understand that the specular image is their own, they develop heightened interest in it. In this way, self-referential pointing may reflect toddlers' tendency to point out their specular image for their mother or the experimenter.

VALIDITY OF THE MARK-AND-MIRROR TEST IN RURAL SOCIOCULTURAL CONTEXTS

One of the main aims of the present study was to evaluate the cross-cultural validity of mirror self-recognition as a measure of toddlers' developing self-awareness and sense of themselves as autonomous agents. In addition to taking into account potential alternative explanations for cross-cultural differences in MSR, we aimed to assess the cross-cultural validity of the mark-and-mirror test by including external criteria. To do so, we analyzed the relation between toddlers' performance in the mark-and-mirror test and maternal reports of toddlers' pronoun and name usage. In line with our hypothesis, we found consistent positive correlations between MSR performance and pronoun/name usage. These correlations were even more pronounced in the rural samples. Taken together, there is sound empirical evidence that MSR is an appropriate indicator of toddlers' developing self-awareness and sense of themselves as autonomous agents, irrespective of the sociocultural context.

ALTERNATIVE EXPLANATIONS OF CROSS-CULTURAL DIFFERENCES IN MSR RATES

In addition to our central hypothesis that cross-cultural differences in MSR are a result of cross-cultural differences in normative sociocultural orientation and socialization goals, we also tested several alternative explanations for these cross-cultural differences. We will address each of these in turn.

Familiarity With Mirrors

We tested the possibility that cross-cultural differences in MSR can be explained in terms of different degrees of mirror familiarity. In the present study, it was not the case that the rural Indian and rural Nso children had never seen a mirror before, as Priel and de Schonen (1986) claim of the Bedouin-nomadic children in their sample. Instead of contrasting children with ample mirror experience to children with no mirror experience at all, in the present study, we contrasted children with very high versus very low degrees of mirror familiarity. Thus, we examined the extent to which the context in which children grow up explains the increase in MSR over consecutive weeks. If mirror familiarity affects performance on the mark-and-mirror test, then the increase in MSR rates over assessment weeks should be significantly higher for toddlers in the rural samples, who initially had very low degrees of mirror familiarity, compared to toddlers in the urban samples.

Contrary to this prediction, the model comparison test was only marginally significant and the goodness-of-fit indices hardly increased when the interaction coefficient (C_{u-r} × week) was added to the stepwise regression model; the difference in MSR rates between the urban and rural samples did not change over successive assessment weeks. In addition, the MSR rates of same-aged toddlers with different degrees of mirror and task familiarity (first vs. fifth and second vs. sixth assessments, respectively) did not differ systematically from each other. Consequently, we arrived at the same conclusion as Priel and de Schonen (1989); the degree of mirror familiarity does not affect mark-directed behavior. Unlike Priel and de Schonen, however, we did expect there to be cross-cultural differences in MSR. From our point of view, these differences can be accounted for by cross-cultural differences in autonomy-supporting socialization practices but not by cross-cultural differences in mirror familiarity. This finding is in line with comparative approaches showing that experience with mirrors has a minimal impact on performance in the mark-and-mirror test (Povinelli et al., 1993).

Norms of Expressive Behavior

Second, we turn to culture-specific norms of expressive behavior as a further potential explanation of cross-cultural differences in MSR. In order to test this possibility, we evaluated cross-cultural differences in (1) latencies to pass the mark-and-mirror test and (2) toddlers' expressive behavior vis-à-vis their specular image. In support of this hypothesis, the rural Nso toddlers had comparably high latencies for passing the mark-and-mirror test. On average, it took these toddlers 42 s to show mark-directed behavior after they first looked at their marked faces, which was about twice as long as it took toddlers' from the two urban settings. Rural Indian toddlers took about 32 s to show mark-directed behavior. This explanation can only partially (if at all) account for the observed cross-cultural differences in MSR, however. If cross-cultural differences in latencies do underpin the cross-cultural differences in MSR, then samples that exhibit higher latencies should also exhibit lower rates of MSR. This was not the case; rural Nso toddlers took longer than rural Indian toddlers to show mark-directed behavior, yet the rural Nso toddlers exhibited higher rates of MSR than did the rural Indian toddlers.

We also examined toddlers' expressive behavior vis-à-vis their specular image to determine whether toddlers in the rural samples were generally less expressive than were toddlers in the autonomy-supporting sociocultural contexts. In this way, toddlers from the rural samples may have had lower MSR rates simply because they have generally reduced rates of expressive behavior. To test this alternative, we examined the frequency and duration of various aspects of the children's behaviors including experimenting, playmate behavior, self-referential pointing, other-referential pointing, getting into the mirror, and looking behind the mirror. In contrast to this assumption, the results of these analyses indicated that toddlers in the rural samples showed the highest frequencies and durations for all behaviors except self-referential pointing and looking behind the mirror.

Motivation for Tactile Exploration

Finally, one could argue that toddlers in the rural sample may simply lack the motivation to explore the mark on their faces. To test this alternative interpretation, we used the marked-hand and the marked-mother task. The marked-hand task was only assessed in the two rural samples and about 75% of toddlers in both samples passed the test, independent of age or gender. Performance in the marked-hand task was correlated with passing the mark-and-mirror test only in the rural Nso sample, however, yielding mixed support for the lack-of-motivation hypothesis. This effect explains cross-cultural differences in MSR rates to only a small extent: First, despite the finding that most toddlers referred to the mark on their hands, only a minority referred to the mark on their face, especially in the rural Indian sample. Second, performance in the marked-hand task was unrelated to MSR in the rural Indian sample. Finally, the MSR pass rates in the subsample of 20- and 21-month-old rural Nso toddlers who passed the marked-hand test still fell below the MSR rates of the 19-month-olds from the urban samples.

Furthermore, findings from the marked-mother task indicate that the motivation to explore a novel mark accounts for a certain proportion of the cross-cultural variation in mirror self-recognition rates. Even if pass rates for the marked-mother task were significantly lower in the rural settings (50%) than in the urban settings (85%), this does not seem to consistently influence toddlers' performance in the mark-and-mirror test. Although there were no significant correlations between toddlers' performance on the marked-mother test and toddlers' cMSR scores, there were two (out of a possible 24) significant correlations between toddlers' performance on the marked-mother task and toddlers' MSR scores. Therefore, we included performance on the marked-mother task as the second predictor (in addition to autonomous socialization goals) in the final logistic regression analyses on mirror self-recognition. The results of this analysis showed that performance on the marked-mother task was significantly and positively associated with MSR and cMSR. It is important to keep in mind, however, that the relative contribution of toddlers' performance in the marked-mother task as an index of their motivation to tactually explore a novel mark was considerably smaller than the contribution of caretakers' autonomous socialization goals.

Finally, one must exercise caution in interpreting the results of the final regression analyses in terms of unraveling the factors that contribute to cross-cultural differences in mirror self-recognition. Despite the minimum requirement that the predictors correlate with mirror self-recognition within at least one of the sociocultural contexts, it is still possible that the predictor—in this case performance in the marked-mother task—is not causally related to toddlers' performance during the MSR assessments. Instead, it is possible that the associated regression coefficients are based on cross-cultural mean differences in both the dependent (MSR and cMSR, respectively) and independent variables (performance in the marked-mother task).

Taken together, the findings from the marked-hand and the marked-mother task seem to indicate that the motivation to explore a novel mark only accounts for a certain, and rather small, proportion of the cross-cultural variation in MSR rates.

CONCLUSION

Our interpretation of the cross-cultural differences in MSR reported here conflicts with the views of most researchers studying MSR (e.g., see Table 1). These researchers argue that there are no specific environmental or social influences on the development of MSR and that its development can mainly be accounted for by maturational processes. This view is largely based on the fact that there are only rare and inconsistent findings concerning relations between MSR and contextual factors, such as family socioeconomic status, parents' level of formal education, or children's gender or birth rank (Asendorpf & Baudonnière, 1993; Asendorpf et al., 1996; Harel et al., 2002; Lewis, Brooks-Gunn, & Jaskir, 1985; Schneider-Rosen & Cicchetti, 1991). As discussed above, these findings stem from studies with very homogeneous samples—mainly urban middle- to upper middle-class families from Western cultural contexts. Given this limitation, we agree with Henrich et al.'s (2010) conclusion that it is highly problematic to generalize results from industrialized populations to humans in general. Similar to our view, Henrich et al.'s main argument is that "different environments, experiences, and cultural routines may encourage reliance on one [cognitive] system at the expense of the other, giving rise to population-level differences in the use of these different cognitive strategies to solve identical problems" (Henrich et al., 2010, p. 72). Any developmental achievement is an environmentally labile process and maturation is an experience-expectant process (Boesch, 2007).

WIDER IMPLICATIONS

The present study has implications for our understanding of development in more general terms by adding one more piece to the emerging picture of culture-specific developmental pathways. This approach conceptualizes development as the culture-specific solution to universal developmental tasks with the goal of developing a self-concept that is adapted to the particular sociocultural environment (Greenfield et al., 2003; Keller, 2007; Rothbaum et al., 2000). Based on the results of the present study, we argue that certain aspects of the sociocultural context, namely caretakers' socialization goals and the parenting practices that they apply, have a systematic and profound influence on children's sociocognitive development. Thus, we argue that this cultural precocity assumption is not restricted to the domain of mirror self-recognition, but systematically affects other developmental domains that are associated with the two basic dimensions that are fundamental to human functioning, namely autonomy and relatedness.

If the cultural precocity assumption is correct, then there should be systematic cross-cultural differences in other developmental domains that are linked to caretakers' broader cultural models. There is some support for this notion; several studies have reported cross-cultural differences in developmental domains that are associated with a cultural emphasis on autonomy. For example, researchers have shown that there is considerable cross-cultural variation in the onset of children's ability to understand or predict others' behavior based on independent mental states attributed to the actor (false belief understanding) (Chasiotis, Kiessling, Hofer, & Campos, 2006; Vinden, 1999, 2002; Wellman et al., 2001). As is the case with the MSR findings reported here, children from sociocultural contexts in which caretakers elaborate on the child's and others' inner states (volitions, emotions, cognitions) show advanced levels of false-belief understanding compared to children from sociocultural contexts with a more relational view of the individual (Symons, 2004). Similarly, Boesch (2007), in his review of cross-cultural differences in false-belief understanding, concluded that:

> Individuals need a phase during their up-bringing during which they face conditions that challenge them for any experience-based ability to develop. Such an "ecological imprint" would select for the development of ability to solve such challenges. If, however, the situations are never or infrequently encountered, experience-based cognitive abilities will remain absent or develop only partially. (p. 235)

One could even go a step further and argue that not only do developmental trajectories (and the consequent onset of specific developmental attainments) differ depending on the sociocultural context, but that the developmental endpoints (i.e., achievements) also differ as a function of the sociocultural context. There is some support for the notion of culture-specific achievements of developmental pathways in at least three developmental domains. First, regarding cultural conceptions of the individual, Miller has shown that even if there are cross-cultural commonalities during childhood (Miller, 1986), Indian participants tend to describe others in terms of references to what they do and where or when it is done, whereas American participants primarily use trait attributions (Miller, 1987). Thus, the development of person description proceeds along contrasting pathways reflective of cultural notions of what constitutes an individual. In this way, context-free trait attributions describe highly autonomous conceptions of others with the abstract individual as the basic social unit, whereas context-bound behavioral descriptions of others are reflective of more relational or sociocentric conceptions, in which the individual is socially constituted.

Second, experimental research has shown that analytical reasoning styles (i.e., a context-free focus on objects' attributes) are more valued and are more prevalent in autonomous sociocultural contexts, whereas holistic reasoning styles (i.e., an orientation to the context or field as a whole) are both more valued and more prevalent in East Asian contexts (i.e., relational sociocultural contexts) (Buchtel & Norenzayan, 2008; Masuda & Nisbett, 2001). Generally, individuals from regions with greater prevalence of relational self-construals exhibit more holistic processing (Uskul, Kitayama, & Nisbett, 2008; Varnum, Grossmann, Katunar, Nisbett, & Kitayama, 2008).

Finally, in the domain of morality development, Miller and colleagues have shown that Euro-Americans and Indians develop along contrasting pathways toward qualitatively distinct interpersonal moral codes (Miller & Bersoff, 1992, 1994). The individually oriented interpersonal moral code of Euro-Americans stresses personal freedom of choice, a contractual view of social relationships, and individual responsibility for action. The duty-based interpersonal moral code typical of Indians, on the other hand, tends to view interpersonal responsibilities as far-reaching in scope and emphasizes a familial view of social relationships as well as the importance of contextual sensitivity. To sum, all of these studies support our theoretical proposal that there are culture-specific developmental pathways that are systematically related to caretakers' broader cultural models and, most importantly, the socialization goals and parenting practices that they apply.

To conclude, the present study supports the idea that there are culture-specific developmental pathways (e.g., autonomous vs. relational) for early sociocognitive and socioemotional development. Although both psychological systems (i.e., autonomy and relatedness) are present in every individual, different environments, experiences, and cultural routines may encourage reliance on one system at the expense of another. This differential reliance on one system over another results in cross-cultural differences in the use of these different psychological systems to solve universal developmental tasks. As a consequence, developmental processes *must* be analyzed in context, especially with reference to the individual's experiences that are systematically linked to their caretakers' socialization goals and agendas. Much more research is needed before the field of developmental psychology can call itself a science that describes, explains, and predicts developmental processes on a global scale.

REFERENCES

Abels, M., Keller, H., Mohite, P., Mankodi, H., Shastri, J., Bhargava, S., et al. (2005). Early socialization contexts and social experiences of infants in rural and urban Gujarat, India. *Journal of Cross-Cultural Psychology*, **36**, 717–738.
Amsterdam, B. (1972). Mirror self-image reactions before age two. *Developmental Psychobiology*, **5**, 297–305.
Asendorpf, J. B., & Baudonnière, P. (1993). Self-awareness and other-awareness: Mirror self-recognition and synchronic imitation among unfamiliar peers. *Developmental Psychology*, **29**, 88–95.
Asendorpf, J. B., Warkentin, V., & Baudonnière, P. (1996). Self-awareness and other-awareness II: Mirror self-recognition, social contingency awareness, and synchronic imitation. *Developmental Psychology*, **32**, 313–321.
Bard, K. A., Todd, B. K., Bernier, C., Love, J., & Leavens, D. A. (2006). Self-awareness in human and chimpanzee infants: What is measured and what is meant by the mark and mirror test? *Infancy*, **9**, 191–219.
Barresi, J., & Moore, C. (1996). Intentional relations and social understanding. *Behavioral and Brain Sciences*, **19**, 107–154.
Barth, J., Povinelli, D. J., & Cant, J. G. H. (2004). Bodily origins of SELF. In D. R. Beike, J. M. Lampinen, & D. A. Behrend (Eds.), *The self and memory* (pp. 11–43). New York: Psychology Press.
Baudonnière, P., Margules, S., Belkhenchir, S., Carn, G., Pépe, F., & Warkentin, V. (2003). A longitudinal and cross-sectional study of the emergence of the symbolic function in children between 15 and 19 months of age: Pretend play, object permanence understanding, and self-recognition. In R. W. Mitchell (Ed.), *Pretending and imagination in animals and children* (pp. 73–90). Cambridge: Cambridge University Press.
Bischof-Köhler, D. (1989). *Spiegelbild und Empathie: Die Anfänge der sozialen Kognition [Reflection and empathy: The beginnings of social cognition]*. Bern, Switzerland: Huber.
Bischof-Köhler, D. (1991). The development of empathy in infants. In M. E. Lamb & H. Keller (Eds.), *Infant development: Perspectives from German-speaking countries* (pp. 245–273). Hillsdale, NJ: Lawrence Erlbaum Associates.
Bischof-Köhler, D. (1994). Selbstobjektivierung und fremdbezogene Emotionen. Identifikation des eigenen Spiegelbildes, Empathie und prosoziales Verhalten im 2 Lebensjahr [Self-recognition, empathy and prosocial behavior in the second year.]. *Zeitschrift für Psychologie*, **202**, 349–377.
Boesch, C. (2007). What makes us human (homo sapiens)? The challenge of cognitive cross-species comparison. *Journal of Comparative Psychology*, **121**, 227–240.
Broesch, T., Callaghan, T., Henrich, J., Murphy, C., & Rochat, P. (2010). Cultural variations in children's mirror self-recognition. *Journal of Cross-Cultural Psychology*, **40**, 1019–1031.

Buchtel, E. E., & Norenzayan, A. (2008). Which should you use, intuition or logic? Cultural differences in injunctive norms about reasoning. *Asian Journal of Social Psychology*, **11**, 264–273.

Chasiotis, A., Kiessling, F., Hofer, J., & Campos, D. (2006). Theory of mind and inhibitory control in three cultures: Conflict inhibition predicts false belief understanding in Germany, Costa Rica and Cameroon. *International Journal of Behavioral Development*, **30**, 249–260.

Chaudhary, N. (2004). *Listening to culture: Constructing reality from everyday talk*. London: Sage.

Cohen, J., Cohen, P., West, S. G., & Aiken, L. S. (2003). *Applied multiple regression/correlation analysis for the behavioral sciences* (3rd ed.). Mahwah, NJ: Lawrence Erlbaum Associates.

Courage, M. L., Edison, S. C., & Howe, M. L. (2004). Variability in the early development of visual self-recognition. *Infant Behavior and Development*, **27**, 509–532.

de Waal, F. B. M. (2008a). Putting the altruism back into altruism: The evolution of empathy. *Annual Review of Psychology*, **59**, 279–300.

de Waal, F. B. M. (2008b). The thief in the mirror. *PLoS Biology*, **6**, 1621–1622.

Demuth, C. (2008). *Talking to infants: How culture is instantiated in early mother-infant interactions. The case of Cameroonian farming Nso and North German middle-class families*. Unpublished doctoral dissertation, University of Osnabrück, Osnabrück, Germany.

Dixon, J. C. (1957). Development of self-recognition. *Journal of Genetic Psychology*, **91**, 251–256.

Gallup, G. G. (1970). Chimpanzees: Self-recognition. *Science*, **167**, 86–87.

Gallup, G. G. (1977). Self recognition in primates: A comparative approach to the bidirectional properties of consciousness. *American Psychologist*, **32**, 329–338.

Gallup, G. G. (1983). Toward a comparative psychology of mind. In R. E. Mellgren (Ed.), *Animal cognition and behaviour* (pp. 473–510). New York: North-Holland.

Gallup, G. G. (1998). Self-awareness and the evolution of social intelligence. *Behavioural Processes*, **42**, 239–247.

Gaskins, S. (1999). Children's daily lives in a Mayan village: A case study of culturally constructed roles and activities. In A. Goncu (Ed.), *Children's engagement in the world: Sociocultural perspectives* (pp. 25–60). New York: Cambridge University Press.

Gaskins, S., Haight, W., & Lancy, D. F. (2006). The cultural construction of play. In S. Gaskins (Ed.), *Play and development: Evolutionary, sociocultural, and functional perspectives* (pp. 179–202). Mahwah, NJ: Lawrence Erlbaum Associates.

Gergely, G., & Watson, J. S. (1996). The social biofeedback theory of parental affect-mirroring: The development of emotional self awareness and self-control in infancy. *International Journal of Psycho-Analysis*, **77**, 1181–1212.

Gergely, G., & Watson, J. S. (1999). Early social-emotional development: Contingency perception and the social-biofeedback model. In P. Rochat (Ed.), *Early socialization* (pp. 101–137). Mahwah, NJ: Lawrence Erlbaum Associates.

Greenfield, P. M., Keller, H., Fuligni, A., & Maynard, A. (2003). Cultural pathways through universal development. *Annual Review of Psychology*, **54**, 461–490.

Harel, J., Eshel, Y., Ganor, O., & Scher, A. (2002). Antecedents of mirror self-recognition of toddlers: Emotional availability, birth order and gender. *Infant Mental Health Journal*, **23**, 293–309.

Hart, D., & Fegley, S. (1994). Social imitation and the emergence of a mental model of self. In S. T. Parker, R. W. Mitchell, & M. L. Boccia (Eds.), *Social imitation and the emergence of a social model of self* (pp. 149–165). New York: Cambridge University Press.

Henrich, J., Heine, S., & Norenzayan, A. (2010). The weirdest people in the world? *Behavioral and Brain Sciences*, **33**, 61–135.

REFERENCES

Herold, K. H., & Akhtar, N. (2008). Imitative learning from a third-party interaction: Relations with self-recognition and perspective taking. *Journal of Experimental Child Psychology*, **101**, 114–123.

Johnson, D. B. (1982). Altruistic behavior and the development of the self in infants. *Merrill-Palmer Quarterly*, **28**, 379–388.

Kagan, J. (1981). *The second year: The emergence of self-awareness.* Cambridge: Harvard University Press.

Kagitçibasi, Ç. (2007). *Family, self, and human development across cultures: Theory and applications* (2nd ed.). Mahwah, NJ: Lawrence Erlbaum Associates.

Kakar, S. (1981). *The inner world.* New Delhi, India: Oxford University Press.

Kärtner, J. (2008). *Einflussgrößen auf die Entwicklung empathischen Erlebens und prosozialen Verhaltens. Eine kulturvergleichende Untersuchung [Influences on the development of empathic concern and prosocial behavior. A cross-cultural study].* Unpublished doctoral dissertation, University of Osnabrück, Germany.

Kärtner, J., Keller, H., & Chaudhary, N. (2010). Cognitive and social influences on early prosocial behavior in two socio-cultural contexts. *Developmental Psychology*, **46**(4), 905–914.

Kärtner, J., Keller, H., & Yovsi, R. (2010). Mother-infant interaction during the first three months: The emergence of culture-specific contingency patterns. *Child Development*, **81**, 540–554.

Keller, H. (2006). Germany: Continuity and change. In J. Georgas, J. Berry, F. Van de Vijver, Ç. Kagitçibasi, & Y. H. Poortinga (Eds.), *Families across cultures* (pp. 327–355). Cambridge, UK: Cambridge University Press.

Keller, H. (2007). *Cultures of infancy.* Mahwah, NJ: Lawrence Erlbaum Associates.

Keller, H., Kärtner, J., Borke, J., Yovsi, R., & Kleis, A. (2005). Parenting styles and the development of the categorical self: A longitudinal study on mirror self-recognition in Cameroonian Nso and German families. *International Journal of Behavioral Development*, **29**, 496–504.

Keller, H., & Otto, H. (2009). The cultural socialization of emotion regulation during infancy. *Journal of Cross-Cultural Psychology*, **40**, 996–1011.

Keller, H., Voelker, S., & Yovsi, R. D. (2005). Conceptions of parenting in different cultural communities: The case of west African Nso and northern German women. *Social Development*, **14**, 158–180.

Keller, H., Yovsi, R., Borke, J., Kärtner, J., Jensen, H., & Papaligoura, Z. (2004). Developmental consequences of early parenting experiences: Self-recognition and self-regulation in three cultural communities. *Child Development*, **75**, 1745–1760.

Keller, H., Yovsi, R. D., & Voelker, S. (2002). The role of motor stimulation in parental ethnotheories: The case of Cameroonian Nso and German women. *Journal of Cross-Cultural Psychology*, **33**, 398–414.

Keller, H., Zach, U., & Abels, M. (2005). The German family: Families in Germany. In J. Roopnarine & U. Gielen (Eds.), *Families in global perspective* (pp. 242–258). Boston: Allyn & Bacon.

Lannoy, R. (1971). *The speaking tree.* London: Oxford University Press.

LeVine, L. E. (1983). Mine: Self-definition in 2-year-old boys. *Developmental Psychology*, **19**, 544–549.

LeVine, R. A., Dixon, S., LeVine, S., Richman, A., Leiderman, P. H., Keefer, C. H., & Brazelton, T. B. (1994). *Childcare and culture: Lessons from Africa.* Cambridge, UK: Cambridge University Press.

LeVine, R. A., & Norman, K. (2001). The infant's acquisition of culture: Early attachment re-examined in anthropological perspective. In C. C. Moore & H. F. Mathews (Eds.), *The psychology of cultural experience* (pp. 83–104). Cambridge, UK: Cambridge University Press.

Lewis, M., & Brooks-Gunn, J. (1979). *Social cognition and the acquisition of self.* New York: Plenum Press.

Lewis, M., Brooks-Gunn, J., & Jaskir, J. (1985). Individual differences in visual self-recognition as a function of mother-infant attachment relationship. *Developmental Psychology*, **21**, 1181–1187.

Lewis, M., & Ramsay, D. S. (1997). Stress reactivity and self-recognition. *Child Development*, **68**, 621–629.

Lewis, M., & Ramsay, D. S. (2004). Development of self-recognition, personal pronoun use, and pretend play during the 2nd year. *Child Development*, **75**, 1821–1831.

Lewis, M., Sullivan, M. W., Stanger, C., & Weiss, M. (1989). Self development and self-conscious emotions. *Child Development*, **60**, 146–156.

Markus, H. R., & Kitayama, S. (1991). Culture and the self: Implications for cognition, emotion, and motivation. *Psychological Review*, **98**, 224–253.

Masuda, T., & Nisbett, R. E. (2001). Attending holistically versus analytically: Comparing the context sensitivity of Japanese and Americans. *Journal of Personality and Social Psychology*, **81**, 922–934.

Meltzoff, A. N. (2007a). "Like me": A foundation for social cognition. *Developmental Science*, **10**, 126–134.

Meltzoff, A. N. (2007b). The "like me" framework for recognizing and becoming an intentional agent. *Acta Psychologica*, **124**, 26–43.

Miller, J. G. (1986). Early cross-cultural commonalities in social explanation. *Developmental Psychology*, **22**, 514–520.

Miller, J. G. (1987). Cultural influences on the development of conceptual differentiation in person description. *British Journal of Developmental Psychology*, **5**, 309–319.

Miller, J. G., & Bersoff, D. M. (1992). Culture and moral judgment: How are conflicts between justice and interpersonal responsibilities resolved? *Journal of Personality and Social Psychology*, **62**, 541–554.

Miller, J. G., & Bersoff, D. M. (1994). Cultural influences on the moral status of reciprocity and the discounting of endogenous motivation. *Personality and Social Psychology Bulletin*, **20**, 592–602.

Miller, J. G., & Bersoff, D. M. (1998). The role of liking in perceptions of the moral responsibility to help: A cultural perspective. *Journal of Experimental Social Psychology*, **34**, 443–469.

Miller, J. G., Bersoff, D. M., & Harwood, R. L. (1990). Perceptions of social responsibilities in India and in the United States: Moral imperatives or personal decisions? *Journal of Personality and Social Psychology*, **58**, 33–47.

Miller, J. G., & Luthar, S. (1989). Issues of interpersonal responsibility and accountability: A comparison of Indians' and Americans' moral judgments. *Social Cognition*, **7**, 237–261.

Mitchell, R. W. (1993). Mental models of mirror-self-recognition: Two theories. *New Ideas in Psychology*, **11**, 295–325.

Moore, C. (2007). Understanding self and others in the second year. In C. A. Brownell & C. B. Kopp (Eds.), *Socioemotional development in the toddler years: Transitions and transformations* (pp. 43–65). New York: Guilford Press.

Moore, C., Mealiea, J., Garon, N., & Povinelli, D. J. (2007). The development of body self-awareness. *Infancy*, **11**, 157–174.

Munroe, R. L., & Munroe, R. H. (1975). Levels of obedience among U.S. and East African children on an experimental task. *Journal of Cross-Cultural Psychology*, **6**, 498–503.

Nielsen, M., & Dissanayake, C. (2004). Pretend play, mirror self-recognition and imitation: A longitudinal investigation through the second year. *Infant Behavior and Development*, **27**, 342–365.

Nielsen, M., Dissanayake, C., & Kashima, Y. (2003). A longitudinal investigation of self-other discrimination and the emergence of mirror self-recognition. *Infant Behavior and Development*, **26**, 213–226.

Nielsen, M., Suddendorf, T., & Slaughter, V. (2006). Mirror self-recognition beyond the face. *Child Development*, **77**, 176–185.

Nsamenang, A. B. (1992). *Human development in cultural context: A third-world perspective.* Newbury Park, CA: Sage.

Ogunnaike, O. A., & Houser, R. F., Jr. (2002). Yoruba toddlers' engagement in errands and cognitive performance on the Yoruba Mental Subscale. *International Journal of Behavioral Development*, **26**, 145–153.

Pampel, F. C. (2000). *Logistic regression: A primer.* Thousand Oaks, CA: Sage.

Perner, J. (1991). *Understanding the representational mind.* London: The MIT Press.

Povinelli, D. J., & Cant, J. G. H. (1995). Arboreal clambering and the evolution of self-conception. *The Quarterly Review of Biology*, **70**, 393–421.

Povinelli, D. J., Rulf, A. B., Landau, K. R., & Bierschwale, D. T. (1993). Self-recognition in chimpanzees (pan troglodytes): Distribution, ontogeny, and patterns of emergence. *Journal of Comparative Psychology*, **107**, 347–372.

Priel, B., & de Schonen, S. (1986). Self-recognition: A study of a population without mirrors. *Journal of Experimental Child Psychology*, **41**, 237–250.

Raman, V. (2003). The diverse life-worlds of Indian childhood. In M. Pernau, I. Ahmad, & H. Reifeld (Eds.), *Family and gender: Changing values in Germany and India* (pp. 84–111). New Delhi, India: Sage.

Repacholi, B. M., & Gopnik, A. (1997). Early reasoning about desires: Evidence from 14- and 18-month-olds. *Developmental Psychology*, **33**, 12–21.

Rochat, P., & Zahavi, D. (2011). The uncanny mirror: A re-framing of mirror self-experience. *Cognition and Consciousness*, **20**, 204–213.

Rothbaum, F., Pott, M., Azuma, H., Miyake, K., & Weisz, J. (2000). The development of close relationships in Japan and the United States: Paths of symbiotic harmony and generative tension. *Child Development*, **71**, 1121–1142.

Sarangapani, P. M. (1999). The child's construction of knowledge. In T. S. Saraswathi (Ed.), *Culture, socialization and human development* (pp. 85–122). New Delhi, India: Sage.

Schneider-Rosen, K., & Cicchetti, D. (1984). The relationship between affect and cognition in maltreated infants: Quality of attachment and the development of visual self-recognition. *Child Development*, **55**, 648–658.

Schneider-Rosen, K., & Cicchetti, D. (1991). Early self-knowledge and emotional development: Visual self-recognition and affective reactions to mirror self-images in maltreated and non-maltreated toddlers. *Developmental Psychology*, **27**, 471–478.

Shweder, K. A., & Bourne, E. J. (1982). Does the concept of person vary cross-culturally? In A. J. Marsella & G. M. White (Eds.), *Cultural conceptions of mental health and therapy* (pp. 97–137). Boston: Reidel.

Sinha, D., & Tripathi, R. C. (1994). Individualism in a collective culture: A case of coexistence of opposites. In U. Kim, H. C. Triandis, Ç. Kagitçibasi, S. Choi, & G. Yoon (Eds.),

Individualism and collectivism: Theory, method and applications (pp. 123–136). Thousand Oaks, CA: Sage.

Suddendorf, T., & Whiten, A. (2001). Mental evolution and development: Evidence for secondary representation in children, great apes, and other animals. *Psychological Bulletin,* **127**, 629–650.

Symons, D. K. (2004). Mental state discourse, theory of mind, and the internalization of self-other understanding. *Developmental Review,* **24**, 159–188.

Thelen, E., & Smith, L. B. (1994). *A dynamic systems approach to the development of cognition and action.* Cambridge: MIT Press.

Tomasello, M. (2008). *Origins of human communication.* Cambridge: MIT Press.

Tomasello, M., Carpenter, M., Call, J., Behne, T., & Moll, H. (2005). Understanding and sharing intentions: The origins of cultural cognition. *Behavioral and Brain Sciences,* **28**, 675–735.

Tomasello, M., & Haberl, K. (2003). Understanding attention: 12- and 18-month-olds know what is new for other persons. *Developmental Psychology,* **39**, 906–912.

Triandis, H. C. (1994). *Culture and social behavior.* New York: McGraw-Hill.

Uskul, A. K., Kitayama, S., & Nisbett, R. E. (2008). Ecocultural basis of cognition: Farmers and fishermen are more holistic than herders. *Proceedings of the National Academy of Sciences USA,* **105**, 8552–8556.

van Geert, P. (1991). A dynamic systems model of cognitive and language growth. *Psychological Review,* **98**, 3–53.

van Geert, P., & van Dijk, M. (2002). Focus on variability: New tools to study intra-individual variability in developmental data. *Infant Behavior and Development,* **25**, 340–374.

Varnum, M. E. W., Grossmann, I., Katunar, D., Nisbett, R. E., & Kitayama, S. (2008). Holism in a European cultural context: Differences in cognitive style between central and east Europeans and westerners. *Journal of Cognition and Culture,* **8**, 321–333.

Verma, S., & Saraswathi, T. S. (2002). Adolescence in India: Street urchins or Silicon Valley millionaires. In B. B. Brown, R. W. Larson, & T. S. Saraswathi (Eds.), *The world's youth: Adolescence in eight regions of the globe* (pp. 105–140). Cambridge, UK: Cambridge University Press.

Vinden, P. G. (1999). Children's understanding of mind and emotion: A multi-culture study. *Cognition and Emotion,* **13**, 19–48.

Vinden, P. G. (2002). Understanding minds and evidence for belief: A study of Mofu children in Cameroon. *International Journal of Behavioral Development,* **26**, 445–452.

Wang, Q., & Chaudhary, N. (2005). The self. In K. Pawlik & G. d'Ydewalle (Eds.), *Psychological concepts: An international historical perspective* (pp. 325–358). Hove, UK: Psychology Press.

Wellman, H. M., Cross, D., & Watson, J. (2001). Meta-analysis of theory-of-mind development: The truth about false belief. *Child Development,* **72**, 655–684.

Whiting, B. B., & Whiting, J. W. (1975). *Children of six cultures: A psycho-cultural analysis.* Cambridge: Harvard University Press.

Yovsi, R. D. (2003). *An investigation of breastfeeding and mother-infant interactions in the face of cultural taboos and belief systems: The case of Nso and Fulani mothers and their infants of 3–5 months of age in Mbvem, subdivision of the northwestern province of Cameroon.* Münster, Germany: Lit.

Zahn-Waxler, C., Radke-Yarrow, M., Wagner, E., & Chapman, M. (1992). Development of concern for others. *Developmental Psychology,* **28**, 126–136.

ACKNOWLEDGMENTS

This study was supported by a grant from the German Research Foundation (DFG) to the second author (KE 263/52–1). Many thanks go to Monika Abels, Pooja Bhargava, Rashi Gupta, Deepa Gupta, Shashi Shukla, and Pooja Vadhera for assessing and coding the rural and urban Indian data. We would also like to thank Eunice Kiyeinimo, Nelly Ayuvea, and Stella Bulami for data collection in Kumbo, Cameroon. Furthermore, we thank Mirjam Böning, Inga Großberndt, and Vanessa Szalma for assessing and coding the German data and Mirjam Böning for helping to coordinate coding and to integrate the data from the different research sites. Finally, we are especially indebted to all the families that participated in this study.

CONTRIBUTORS

Joscha Kärtner received his Ph.D. from the Department of Culture and Development at the University of Osnabrück, Germany. He presently holds a postdoctoral research position at the nifbe-research unit Development, Learning, and Culture at the University of Osnabrück. His research interests include early mother–infant interaction in different cultures and sociocognitive and socioemotional development across cultures.

Heidi Keller received her Ph.D. from the University of Mainz, Germany, and is a professor of Psychology, head of the Department of Culture and Development, and head of the nifbe-research unit Development, Learning, and Culture at the University of Osnabrück. Her research interests include the interplay between culture and biology, the development of cultural pathways through universal developmental tasks, and culturally informed child-care programs and family counseling.

Nandita Chaudhary received her Ph.D. from the University of Delhi and is presently employed as a Professor at the Department of Human Development and Childhood Studies, Lady Irwin College, University of Delhi. Her main research interests are in the area of culture, children's development, and family studies. During her career, she has been an advisor to several national and international agencies (Governmental, Nongovernmental, and community).

Relindis D. Yovsi earned her Ph.D. from the Department of Culture and Development from the University of Osnabrück. She has worked as a research fellow in the same department. Her areas of interest include parenting in cross-cultural context, infant feeding, immigration, children under nonparental care, and status and role of children in traditional communities. She is a consultant on infant feeding and maternal and infant care.

STATEMENT OF EDITORIAL POLICY

The SRCD *Monographs* series aims to publish major reports of developmental research that generates authoritative new findings and that foster a fresh perspective and/or integration of data/research on conceptually significant issues. Submissions may consist of individually or group-authored reports of findings from some single large-scale investigation or from a series of experiments centering on a particular question. Multiauthored sets of independent studies concerning the same underlying question also may be appropriate. A critical requirement in such instances is that the individual authors address common issues and that the contribution arising from the set as a whole be unique, substantial, and well integrated. Manuscripts reporting interdisciplinary or multidisciplinary research on significant developmental questions and those including evidence from diverse cultural, racial, and ethnic groups are of particular interest. Also of special interest are manuscripts that bridge basic and applied developmental science, and that reflect the international perspective of the Society. Because the aim of the *Monographs* series is to enhance cross-fertilization among disciplines or subfields as well as advance knowledge on specialized topics, the links between the specific issues under study and larger questions relating to developmental processes should emerge clearly and be apparent for both general readers and specialists on the topic. In short, irrespective of how it may be framed, work that contributes significant data and/or extends a developmental perspective will be considered.

Potential authors who may be unsure whether the manuscript they are planning would make an appropriate submission to the SRCD *Monographs* are invited to draft an outline or prospectus of what they propose and send it to the incoming editor for review and comment.

Potential authors are not required to be members of the Society for Research in Child Development nor affiliated with the academic discipline of psychology to submit a manuscript for consideration by the *Monographs*. The significance of the work in extending developmental theory and in contributing new empirical information is the crucial consideration.

Submissions should contain a minimum of 80 manuscript pages (including tables and references). The upper boundary of 150–175 pages is more flexible, but authors should try to keep within this limit. If color artwork is submitted, and the authors believe color art is necessary to the presentation of their work, the submissions letter should indicate that one or more authors or their institutions are prepared to pay the substantial costs associated with color art reproduction. Please submit manuscripts electronically to the SRCD Monographs Online Submissions and Review Site (Scholar One) at http://mc.manuscriptcentral.com/mono. Please contact the Monographs office with any questions at monographs@srcd.org.

The corresponding author for any manuscript must, in the submission letter, warrant that all coauthors are in agreement with the content of the manuscript. The corresponding author also is responsible for informing all coauthors, in a timely manner, of manuscript submission, editorial decisions, reviews received, and any revisions recommended. Before publication, the corresponding author must warrant in the submissions letter that the study has been conducted according to the ethical guidelines of the Society for Research in Child Development.

A more detailed description of all editorial policies, evaluation processes, and format requirements, is given in the "Guidelines for the Preparation of Publication Submissions," which can be found at the SRCD website by clicking on *Monographs*, or by contacting the editor.

Monographs Editorial Office
e-mail: monographs@srcd.org

Incoming Editor, Patricia J. Bauer
Department of Psychology, Emory University
36 Eagle Row
Atlanta, GA 30322
e-mail: pjbauer@emory.edu

Note to NIH Grantees

Pursuant to NIH mandate, Society through Wiley-Blackwell will post the accepted version of Contributions authored by NIH grantholders to PubMed Central upon acceptance. This accepted version will be made publicly available 12 months after publication. For further information, see http://www.wiley.com/go/nihmandate.

SUBJECT INDEX

Page numbers in *italics* refer to figures and tables.

age of emergence (AOE), vii, 7, 8–9, 21, 22, 66, 69–70
Athens, Greece, 13
autonomy, vii, 7, 12, 13, 15, 68, 69
autonomy-relational culture, 12–13, 15, 17, 22, 47. *See also* Indian (urban) Sociocultural Context
autonomy-supporting culture. *See also* German Sociocultural Context; Indian (urban) Sociocultural Context
    age of emergence, 22, 67
    age of mother, 27
    assertiveness, 46
    contractual view of social relationships, 10
    cultural models, 10–11, 12, 13
    education patterns, 11, 27, 77
    experimenting behavior, 9–10
    freedom of choice, 10
    individual agent, 10, 11, 12, 14–15, 46, 62, 66, 67
    marked behavior, 72
    maternal socialization goals, 61, 62
    mirror familiarity, 75
    personal interest, 46
    personal preferences, 46
    personal responsibility, 10, 17
    playmate behavior, 9–10
    self-recognition development, 48, 61, 62, 72
    socialization goals, vii, 15, 17, 29–30, 46–47, 61, 62, 63–65, 66, 68, 72
    socioeconomic patterns, 11, 77
Bedouin-nomadic families, 13
behavior, expressive
  across time, 56–59
  cross-cultural differences, 15, 23, 56–59, 61
  culture-specific norms, vii
  norms, 20, 21, 75–76
  specular image, vii, 9–10, 21, 22, 53–59, 66, 73–74, 75–76
Catholic religion, 25, 26
cultural precocity assumption, 12, 13, 14, 78

culture-specific developmental pathways, 10, 66–68, 78
    critical age span for MSR, 24
    cultural models, 10–11
    culture and development, 11–12
    culture and self-concept, 12–14
    development of morality, 12
    development of person, 79
    false-belief understanding, 12, 78
    family structure, 11, 27
    everyday routines, 11
    logistic regression analyses, 47–50
    mechanisms underlying, 68–69
    mother's age, 11, 27
    number of siblings, 11, 27, 77
    person perception, 12
    socialization goals, 12, 13–14, 46–47, 67, 78, 79
    subsistence patterns, 11
cumulative self-recognizer. *See* self-recognizer

dyadic interaction, 16

education. *See* autonomy-supporting culture; relational culture; *specific cultural group*
embarrassment (self-conscious emotion), 1, 6–7
experimenting behavior. *See* mirror, familiarity with

family visits and MSR assessments, 27, 28

gender differences, 66. *See also* mirror self-recognition
    in Nso families, 19–20
    study participants, 27, 77
    work, 17–18
German Sociocultural Context. *See also* autonomy-supporting culture
    age of emergence, 14, 22–23, 52, 70, 71
    assessment week and cMSR rates, 45
    autonomy orientation, 15, 16, 46, 47
    critical age span for MSR, 24
    dyadic interaction, 16
    education, 16, 25
    experimenting behavior, 9–10, 57
    expressive behavior compared to Nso toddlers, 53–59, *54*
    false localization behavior, 41
    family role distribution, 16
    gender and MSR rates, 45
    getting into mirror, 59
    households, 27
    incidence of mirror behavior, 56–57
    individual agent, 16, 67
    looking behind mirror, 59

SUBJECT INDEX

mark-directed behavior, *42*, 42, 54, 72
marked-mother assessment, 61
MSR and cMSR rates, 43–45, *44*, 62
obedience, 67
playmate behavior, 9–10, 58, 73
pronoun use and self-recognition, 50
referential pointing, 59
religious affiliation, 25
self-recognizer trends, 37, *38*, 39–41, *39*, *40*, 48, 65
self-reliance, 16
socialization goals, 46–47, *47*, 66, 67
sociodemographic information, *28*
socioeconomic context, vii, 16, 25
study selection, 16, 25

Hindus, 16, 17, 25, 26

Indian (rural) Sociocultural Context. *See also* relational culture
age of emergence, 23, 52, 70, 71
assessment week and cMSR rates, 45
children's activities, 18
compliance, 18
critical age span for MSR, 24
dutifulness, 19
education, 17, 18, 26
experimenting behavior, 57
false localization behavior, 41
gender divisions in work, 17–18
households, 27
incidence of mirror behavior, 56–57
looking behind mirror, 59
male family members, 18
mark-directed behavior, *42*, 70, 72, 74, 75
marked-hand assessment, 59
marked-mother assessment, 61
mirror familiarity, 74
moral code, 79
MSR and cMSR rates, 15–16, 43–45, *44*, 62, 72–73
MSR stability, 72
"multiple parenting," 18
nonrecognizers, 72
obedience, 19, 47
patriarchal family system, 18
playmate behavior, 58, 73
pronoun use and self-recognition, 50
referential pointing, 59
relational orientation, 47
religious affiliation, 26

    respect for elders, 19, 47
    self-recognizer trends, 37, *38*, 39–41, *39*, *40*, 65
    socialization goals, 19, 46–47, *47*
    sociodemographic information, *28*
    socioeconomic context, vii, 26
    study selection, 17–19, 25–26
    tactile exploration, 76
Indian (urban) Sociocultural Context. *See also* autonomy-relational culture; autonomy-supporting culture
    age of emergence, 22–23, 52, 70
    assessment week and cMSR rates, 45
    autonomous-relational orientation, 47
    critical age span for MSR, 24
    education, 17, 25
    experimenting behavior, 57
    false localization behavior, 41
    households, 27
    incidence of mirror behavior, 56–57
    interpersonal responsibilities, 17
    looking behind mirror, 59
    mark-directed behavior, *42*, 72
    marked-mother assessment, 61
    moral code, 79
    MSR rates, 43–45, *44*
    obedience, 67
    outdoor play, 16
    personal talents/interests, 47, 67
    playmate behavior, 58
    pronoun use and self-recognition, 50
    referential pointing, 59
    religious affiliation, 25
    respectful/sensitivity to others, 17
    self-recognizer trends, 37, *38*, 39–41, *39*, *40*, 44, 48, 65
    share with others, 47
    socialization goals, 46–47, *47*, 66, 67
    social relationships, 17
    sociodemographic information, *28*
    socioeconomic context, vii, 16, 17, 25
    study selection, 16–17, 25
intentional schema, 6–7

kinesthetic information, 7, 8

mark-directed behavior, 1, 8, 53, 54, 70, 72
    development of MSR, 41–43
    false localization, 33, 41–42
    latencies, 33, 43, 75
    localization, 33, 41–42

marked-hand, 22, 25, 29, 32, 36, 59–60, 76–77
marked-mother, 22, 25, 29, 32, 35–36, 60–61, 63–65, 76–77
mirror familiarity, 10, 13
showing (turning to another), 33, 41
validity in rural contexts, 74
mirror, familiarity with, vii, 10, 20–21
    compared to secondary representation, 8
    cross-cultural differences, 15, 23 61, 74–75
    experimenting behavior, vii, 9–10, 21, 22, 31, 34–35, 55, 56, 57, 73, 75, 76
    gazing, 22, 31, 34–35, 53–54
    getting into, 9, 33–34, 55, 56, 59, 76
    looking behind, 9, 33–34, 55, 56, 59, 76
    playmate, vii, 9, 10, 21, 22, 31, 34–35, 55, 56, 57–58, 73
    pointing, vii, 10, 21, 22, 31, 34–35, 56, 58–59, 73, 76
    recognition status, 51–52
    touching with face, 33–34, 55
mirror self-recognition (MSR). *See also* age of emergence; gender differences; tactile exploration
    age trends, *3–5*, 9, 20–22, *38*, 43–45, *44*, 46, 52, 66, 67, 72
    assessments, 30, 33–34
    assessment week, 43–45, *44*, 46, 48, *49*, 50, 66
    body self-awareness, 2, 6
    course of, 22
    critical age span, 24
    cross-cultural difference in development, 46–50
    cross-cultural validity, 50–51
    cross-cultural variation, vii–viii, 13, 15, 46–50, 61–65, 67, 74–77
    cumulative self-recognizer (cMSR), 37, *38*, 39–41, *39*, *40*, 44
    developmental trajectories, 37–43, *38*, *40*
    divergence of scores, 70–73
    early self-concept indicator, 2, 8, 12, 23
    gender, 8, 43–45, *44*, 66
    interindividual and cross-cultural differences, 61–65
    logistic regression analyses, 43–50
    meaning of, 2, *3–5*, 6–7
    mirror familiarity, 20–21, 51–52
    mirror image—relation to recognition status/sociocultural context, 53–59
    mirror self-recognition differences, 61–65
    mother–infant interaction, 14
    ontogentic development, 8–9
    pronoun use, vii, 6, 15, 22, 23, 50, *51*
    prosocial behavior, 6
    secondary representation, 7–8
    self-conscious emotions, 1, 6
    Sociocultural Context, 47–50, 52

    sociocultural differences, vii
    social imitation, 6
    stability across weeks, 22, 45–46, 66, 70–73
    status, 33
    synchronous imitation, 6
    testing alternative explanations, 20–22
Negev region (Israel), 13
non-recognizer status, 33, 72
Nso Sociocultural Context. *See also* relational culture
    age of emergence, 14, 23, 52, 70, 71
    assessment week and cMSR rates, 45
    compliance, 20
    critical age span for MSR, 24
    dutifulness, 20
    education, 19, 26
    experimenting behavior, 9–10, 57
    expressive behavior, 21
    expressive behavior compared to German toddlers, 53–59, *54*
    extended family system, 20, 27
    firstborn children, 27
    gender divisions, 19–20
    households, 27
    housing, 19
    incidence of mirror behavior, 56–57
    looking-at/touching mark latencies, 43
    looking behind mirror, 59
    mark-directed behavior, *42*, 70, 74, 75
    marked-hand assessment, 59
    marked-mother assessment, 61
    mirror familiarity, 14, 74
    MSR rates, 15–16, 43–45, *44*, 72–73
    MSR stability, 72
    obedience, 20, 47
    patrilocal settlement pattern, 19–20, 27
    playmate behavior, 9–10, 58, 73
    pronoun use and self-recognition, 50
    referential pointing, 59
    relational orientation, 47
    religious affiliation, 26
    self-recognizer trends, 37, *38*, 39–41, *39*, *40*, 44, 65
    respect for elders, 47
    socialization goals, 46–47, *47*, 72
    sociodemographic information, *28*
    socioeconomic context, vii, 13, 19, 26
    study selection, 19–20, 26
    tactile exploration, 76

one-point-in-time approach, 15
playmate. *See* mirror, familiarity with
pointing. *See* mirror, familiarity with
pretend play, 7
pronoun use. *See* mirror self-recognition

questionnaires (study), 25, 29–30

relational culture. *See also* Indian (rural) Sociocultural Context; Nso Sociocultural Context
    age of mother, 27
    binding interpersonal responsibilities, 10–11
    cultural models, 10–11
    duty-based role obligations, 10, 11
    education patterns, 11, 77
    extended family, 11
    mark-directed behavior, 13
    MSR rates, vii, 15–16
    obedience, 46
    respect for elders, 46
    self-recognition development, 48
    social harmony, 46
    social hierarchical structures, 10, 11
    socialization goals, 29–30, 46–47
    socioeconomic patterns, 11, 77
    traditional values, 11

Saharan culture, 12
San Jose, Costa Rica, 13
secondary representation concept, 6–8
self-awareness, 1, 2, 6–7, 68, 71–72
self-concept, 10, 12–14
self-other differentiation, 1, 6–7, 10
self-recognizer. *See* mirror self-recognition
sociocognitive development, 12, 78
study, 14–23
    methodology, 24–36, 28
    results, 37–65, 77–80

tactile exploration
    cross-cultural differences, 15, 23, 59–61
    motivation, vii, 20, 21–22, 62–63, 67, 76–77
toddler development, 1–7, 9
    attention to internal state, 68–69
    culture-specific pathways, 10–14
    tracing trajectories, 15, 37–41
    triadic interaction, 69

visual-kinesthetic matching, 7

AUTHOR INDEX

Adam, Emma K. Emotion-Cortisol Transactions Occur over Multiple Time Scales in Development: Implications for Research on Emotion and the Development of Emotional Disorders, *Monographs of the Society for Research in Child Development,* 77(2, Serial No. 303), 17–27

Adam, Emma K. *See* Gunnar, Megan R.

Beale, Karen S. *See* Parker, Alison E.

Beauchaine, Theodore P. Physiological Markers of Emotion and Behavior Dysregulation in Externalizing Psychopathology, *Monographs of the Society for Research in Child Development,* 77 (2, Serial No. 303), 79–86

Bell, Martha Ann; & Diaz, Anjolii. EEG/ERP Measures of Emotion-Cognition Integration During Development, *Monographs of the Society for Research in Child Development,* 77(2, Serial No. 303), 8–16

Boldt, Benjamin R. *See* Chian-Hui Chen, Eva

Boyce, W. Thomas *See* Obradović, Jelena

Bryant, Alfred, Jr. *See* Parker, Alison E.

Buss, Kristin A. *See* Dennis, Tracy A.

Buss, Kristin A. *See* Dennis, Tracy A.

Buss, Kristin A. *See* Hastings, Paul D.

Buss, Kristin A. *See* Hastings, Paul D.

Buss, Kristin A.; Hastings, Paul D.; & Dennis, Tracy A. Introduction to Section Three: Physiology and Affective Psychopathology, *Monographs of the Society for Research in Child Development,* 77 (2, Serial No. 303), 67–68

Chaudhary, Nandita *See* Kärtner, Joscha

Chian-Hui Chen, Eva; Miller, Peggy J.; Fung, Heidi; & Boldt, Benjamin R. Interpretive Frameworks in Routine Practices, *Monographs of the Society for Research in Child Development,* 77 (1, Serial No. 302), 28–58

Chian-Hui Chen, Eva *See* Fung, Heidi

Chian-Hui Chen, Eva *See* Lin, Shumin

Chian-Hui Chen, Eva *See* Miller, Peggy J.

Cicchetti, Dante; & Rogosch, Fred A. Neuroendocrine Regulation and Emotional Adaptation in the Context of Child Maltreatment, *Monographs of the Society for Research in Child Development,* 77 (2, Serial No. 303), 87–95

Dahl, Ronald E.; Silk, Jennifer S.; & Siegle, Greg J. Physiological

AUTHOR INDEX

Measures of Emotion Dysregulation: Investigating the Development of Affective Disorders, *Monographs of the Society for Research in Child Development*, 77(2, Serial No. 303), 69–78

Dennis, Tracy A. *See* Buss, Kristin A.

Dennis, Tracy A. *See* Hastings, Paul D.

Dennis, Tracy A.; Buss, Kristin A.; & Hastings, Paul D. Introduction to the Monograph: Physiological Measures of Emotion from a Developmental Perspective: State of the Science, *Monographs of the Society for Research in Child Development*, 77(2, Serial No. 303), 1–5

Dennis, Tracy A.; Buss, Kristin A.; & Hastings, Paul D. (2012). Physiological Measures of Emotion From a Developmental Perspective: State of the Science, *Monographs of the Society for Research in Child Development*, 77(2, Serial No. 303).

Dennis, Tracy A.; Hastings, Paul D.; & Buss, Kristin A. Introduction to Section Four: Overarching Issues and Methodological Considerations: What Can Physiological Measures Reveal about Emotion? *Monographs of the Society for Research in Child Development*, 77(2, Serial No. 303), 96–97

Diaz, Anjolii *See* Bell, Martha Ann

Dunsmore, Julie C. *See* Parker, Alison E.

Feldman, Ruth. Parent-Infant Synchrony: A Biobehavioral Model of Mutual Influences in the Formation of Affiliative Bonds, *Monographs of the Society for Research in Child Development*, 77 (2, Serial No. 303), 42–51

Fox, Nathan A.; Kirwan, Michael; & Reeb-Sutherland, Bethany. Measuring the Physiology of Emotion and Emotion Regulation–Timing is Everything, *Monographs of the Society for Research in Child Development*, 77 (2, Serial No. 303), 98–108

Fung, Heidi *See* Chian-Hui Chen, Eva

Fung, Heidi *See* Lin, Shumin

Fung, Heidi *See* Miller, Peggy J.

Fung, Heidi; Miller, Peggy J.; Lin, Shumin; & Chian-Hui Chen, Eva. Studying Personal Storytelling in Taipei and Longwood, *Monographs of the Society for Research in Child Development*, 77 (1, Serial No. 302), 15–27

Gates, Kathleen M. *See* Molenaar, Peter C. M.

Gunnar, Megan R. & Adam, Emma K. The Hypothalamic–Pituitary–Adrenocortical System and Emotion: Current Wisdom and Future Directions, *Monographs of the Society for Research in Child Development*, 77(2, Serial No. 303), 109–119

Halberstadt, Amy G. *See* Parker, Alison E.

Hanson, Jamie L. *See* Strang, Nicole M.

Hastings, Paul D. *See* Buss, Kristin A.

Hastings, Paul D. *See* Dennis, Tracy A.

Hastings, Paul D.; Buss, Kristin A.; & Dennis, Tracy A. Introduction to Section One: Integrative Approaches to the Study of Physiology and Emotion, *Monographs of the Society for*

Research in Child Development, 77 (2, Serial No. 303), 6–7
Hastings, Paul D.; Buss, Kristin A.; & Dennis, Tracy A. Introduction to Section Two: Socialization and Environmental Factors in the Physiology of Emotion, *Monographs of the Society for Research in Child Development,* 77 (2, Serial No. 303), 39–41

Kärtner, Joscha; Keller, Heidi; Chaudhary, Nandita; & Yovsi, Relindis D. (2012). The Development of Mirror Self-Recognition in Different Sociocultural Contexts, *Monographs of the Society for Research in Child Development,* 77 (4, Serial No. 305)
Katz, Lynn Fainsilber; & Rigterink, Tami. Domestic Violence and Emotion Socialization, *Monographs of the Society for Research in Child Development,* 77 (2, Serial No. 303), 52–60
Keller, Heidi *See* Kärtner, Joscha
Kirwan, Michael *See* Fox, Nathan A.

Lin, Shumin *See* Fung, Heidi
Lin, Shumin *See* Miller, Peggy J.
Lin, Shumin; Miller, Peggy J.; Fung, Heidi; & Chian-Hui Chen, Eva. Participant Roles, *Monographs of the Society for Research in Child Development,* 77(1, Serial No. 302), 59–76

Miller, Peggy J. *See* Chian-Hui Chen, Eva
Miller, Peggy J. *See* Fung, Heidi
Miller, Peggy J. *See* Lin, Shumin
Miller, Peggy J.; Lin, Shumin; Chian-Hui Chen, Eva; & Fung, Heidi. Children Navigating Stories, *Monographs of the Society for Research in Child Development,* 77 (1, Serial No. 302), 77–104
Miller, Peggy J.; & Fung, Heidi. Introduction, *Monographs of the Society for Research in Child Development,* 77(1, Serial No. 302), 1–14
Miller, Peggy J.; Fung, Heidi; Lin, Shumin; Chen, Eva Chian-Hui; & Boldt, Benjamin R. (2012). How Socialization Happens on the Ground: Narrative Practices as Alternate Socializing Pathways in Taiwanese and European-American Families, *Monographs of the Society for Research in Child Development,* 77(1, Serial No. 302)
Miller, Peggy J.; & Lin, Shumin. Discussion, *Monographs of the Society for Research in Child Development,* 77(1, Serial No. 302), 105–114
Miskovic, Vladimir; & Schmidt, Louis A. New Directions in the Study of Individual Differences in Temperament: A Brain-Body Approach to Understanding Fearful and Fearless Children, *Monographs of the Society for Research in Child Development,* 77 (2, Serial No. 303), 28–38
Molenaar, Peter C. M.; & Gates, Kathleen M. Aspects of Psychophysiological Data Analysis: EEG Coherency and fMRI Connectivity Mapping, *Monographs of the Society for Research in Child Development,* 77(2, Serial No. 303), 129–138

Obradović, Jelena; & Boyce, W. Thomas. Developmental Psychophysiology of Emotion Processes, *Monographs of the Society*

AUTHOR INDEX

for Research in Child Development, 77(2, Serial No. 303), 120–128

Parker, Alison E.; Halberstadt, Amy G.; Dunsmore, Julie C.; Townley, Greg; Bryant, Alfred, Jr.; Thompson, Julie A.; & Beale, Karen S. (2012). "Emotions Are a Window Into One's Heart": A Qualitative Analysis of Parental Beliefs About Children's Emotions Across Three Ethnic Groups, *Monographs of the Society for Research in Child Development,* 77(3, Serial No. 304)

Pollak, Seth D. *See* Strang, Nicole M.

Reeb-Sutherland, Bethany *See* Fox, Nathan A.

Rigterink, Tami *See* Katz, Lynn Fainsilber

Rogosch, Fred A. *See* Cicchetti, Dante

Schmidt, Louis A. *See* Miskovic, Vladimir

Siegle, Greg J. *See* Dahl, Ronald E.

Silk, Jennifer S. *See* Dahl, Ronald E.

Strang, Nicole M.; Hanson, Jamie L.; & Pollak, Seth D. The Importance of Biological Methods in Linking Social Experience with Social and Emotional Development, *Monographs of the Society for Research in Child Development,* 77(2, Serial No. 303), 61–66

Thompson, Julie A. *See* Parker, Alison E.

Townley, Greg *See* Parker, Alison E.

Yovsi, Relindis D. *See* Kärtner, Joscha

CURRENT

The Development of Mirror Self-Recognition in Different Sociocultural Contexts—*Joscha Kärtner, Heidi Keller, Nandita Chaudhary, and Relindis D. Yovsi* (SERIAL NO. 305, 2012)

"Emotions Are a Window Into One's Heart": A Qualitative Analysis of Parental Beliefs About Children's Emotions Across Three Ethnic Groups—*Alison E. Parker, Amy G. Halberstadt, Julie C. Dunsmore, Greg Townley, Alfred Bryant, Jr., Julie A. Thompson, and Karen S. Beale* (SERIAL NO. 304, 2012)

Physiological Measures of Emotion From a Developmental Perspective: State of the Science—*Tracy A. Dennis, Kristin A. Buss, and Paul D. Hastings* (SERIAL NO. 303, 2012)

How Socialization Happens on the Ground: Narrative Practices as Alternate Socializing Pathways in Taiwanese and European-American Families—*Peggy J. Miller, Heidi Fung, Shumin Lin, Eva Chian-Hui Chen, and Benjamin R. Boldt* (SERIAL NO. 302, 2012)

Children Without Permanent Parents: Research, Practice, and Policy—*Robert B. McCall, Marinus H. van IJzendoorn, Femmie Juffer, Christina J. Groark, and Victor K. Groza* (SERIAL NO. 301, 2011)

I Remember Me: Mnemonic Self-Reference Effects in Preschool Children—*Josephine Ross, James R. Anderson, and Robin N. Campbell* (SERIAL NO. 300, 2011)

Early Social Cognition in Three Cultural Contexts—*Tara Callaghan, Henrike Moll, Hannes Rakoczy, Felix Warneken, Ulf Liszkowski, Tanya Behne, and Michael Tomasello* (SERIAL NO. 299, 2011)

The Development of Ambiguous Figure Perception—*Marina C. Wimmer and Martin J. Doherty* (SERIAL NO. 298, 2011)

The Better Beinnings, Better Futures Project: Findings From Grade 3 to Grade 9—*Ray DeV. Peters, Alison J. Bradshaw, Kelly Petrunka, Geoffrey Nelson, Yves Herry, Wendy M. Craig, Robert Arnold, Kevin C. H. Parker, Shahriar R. Khan, Jeffrey S. Hoch, S. Mark Pancer, Colleen Loomis, Jean-Marc Bélanger, Susan Evers, Claire Maltais, Katherine Thompson, and Melissa D. Rossiter* (SERIAL NO. 297, 2010)

First-Year Maternal Employment and Child Development in the First 7 Years—*Jeanne Brooks- Gunn, Wen-Jui Han, and Jane Waldfogel* (SERIAL NO. 296, 2010)

Deprivation-Specific Psychological Patterns: Effects of Institutional Deprivation—*Michael Rutter, Edmund J. Sonuga-Barke, Celia Beckett, Jennifer Castle, Jana Kreppner, Robert Kumsta, Wolff Schlotz, Suzanne Stevens, and Christopher A. Bell* (SERIAL NO. 295, 2010)

A Dynamic Cascade Model of the Development of Substance-Use Onset—*Kenneth A. Dodge, Patrick S. Malone, Jennifer E. Lansford, Shari Miller, Gregory S. Pettit, and John E. Bates* (SERIAL NO. 294, 2009)

Flexibility in Early Verb Use: Evidence From a Multiple-*N* Diary Study—*Letitia R. Naigles, Erika Hoff, and Donna Vear* (SERIAL NO. 293, 2009)

Marital Conflict and Children's Externalizing Behavior: Interactions Between Parasympathetic and Sympathetic Nervous System Activity—*Mona El-Sheikh, Chrystyna D. Kouros, Stephen Erath, E. Mark Cummings, Peggy Keller, and Lori Staton* (SERIAL NO. 292, 2009)

The Effects of Early Social-Emotional and Relationship Experience on the Development of Young Orphanage Children—*The St. Petersburg–USA Orphanage Research Team* (SERIAL NO. 291, 2008)

Understanding Mother-Adolescent Conflict Discussions: Concurrent and Across-Time Prediction From Youths' Dispositions and Parenting—*Nancy Eisenberg, Claire Hofer, Tracy L. Spinrad, Elizabeth T. Gershoff, Carlos Valiente, Sandra Losoya, Qing Zhou, Amanda Cumberland, Jeffrey Liew, Mark Reiser, and Elizabeth Maxon* (SERIAL NO. 290, 2008)

Developing Object Concepts in Infancy: An Associative Learning Perspective—*David H. Rakison and Gary Lupyan* (SERIAL NO. 289, 2008)

The Genetic and Environmental Origins of Learning Abilities and Disabilities in the Early School Years—*Yulia Kovas, Claire M. A. Haworth, Philip S. Dale, and Robert Plomin* (SERIAL NO. 288, 2007)

The Preservation of Two Infant Temperaments Into Adolescence—*Jerome Kagan, Nancy Snidman, Vali Kahn, and Sara Towsley* (SERIAL NO. 287, 2007)